meditation & Chri...

Transformed
by the
Beloved

Text copyright © Daniel Muñoz 2014
The author asserts the moral right
to be identified as the author of this work

Published by
The Bible Reading Fellowship
15 The Chambers, Vineyard
Abingdon OX14 3FE
United Kingdom
Tel: +44 (0)1865 319700
Email: enquiries@brf.org.uk
Website: www.brf.org.uk
BRF is a Registered Charity

ISBN 978 1 84101 584 2

First published 2014

10 9 8 7 6 5 4 3 2 1 0

Acknowledgments

Unless otherwise indicated, scripture quotations are taken from The Holy Bible, New
International Version (Anglicised edition) Copyright © 1979, 1984, 2011 by Biblica (formerly
International Bible Society), and are used by permission of Hodder & Stoughton Publishers, an
Hachette UK company. All rights reserved. 'NIV' is a registered trademark of Biblica (formerly
International Bible Society). UK trademark number 1448790.

Scripture quotations taken from The New Revised Standard Version of the Bible, Anglicised
edition, copyright © 1989, 1995 by the Division of Christian Education of the National
Council of the Churches of Christ in the United States of America, are used by permission. All
rights reserved.

Extracts from the Authorised Version of the Bible (The King James Bible), the rights in which
are vested in the Crown, are reproduced by permission of the Crown's Patentee, Cambridge
University Press/

Cover photos: (Sky) Santiago Bañón/Getty Images; (Statue) Photograph by Guy Wynter,
sculpture by Daphne Tengbergen.

A catalogue record for this book is available from the British Library

Printed and bound by CPI Group (UK) Ltd, Croydon CR0 4YY

Transformed by the Beloved

A guide to spiritual formation with
St John of the Cross

Daniel Muñoz

Preface

Much has been written about spiritual formation in recent years, primarily by US authors. In addition, over the past decade, there has been an increasing interest in the Christian mystics, among them the Spanish John of the Cross. In that time, a few interesting studies have been published in the UK, exploring different aspects of John's life and works, some of which are cited in this book. *Transformed by the Beloved* seeks to be a contribution to that growing collection of works, from the perspective of Christian spirituality. It is also a new resource for those who are keen to go deeper in their relationship with God. In this sense, this book seeks to be a guide to spiritual formation and transformation.

I first came across John's poetry when I was 17. It was a compulsory part of my A Level Spanish literature syllabus. I was mildly interested in his poetry, though not so sure about his religious ideas. So, when I went to university, I forgot all about John and his works. Years later, just before my ordination, I was given a copy of St John of the Cross's complete works as a gift for my priesting. Again, my first reaction was not particularly enthusiastic, and I decided to place the thick volume reverently at the top of my bookshelves. There, at least, it would look good yet harm or confuse no one. After all, I was a 21st-century Protestant minister, and Juan de la Cruz, as he is known in Spanish, was a 16th-century Catholic priest. The only thing I felt we had in common was our nationality: we were both Spaniards.

A number of years later, during one of the driest spiritual

deserts of my life, I felt prompted to rescue the dusty old book from the top shelf. I secretly hoped to find in it a quick and easy fix for my personal dark(ish) night of the soul. As I read John's poems, familiarised myself again with his life and immersed myself in his commentaries, I was drawn more and more into the world of the Spanish mystic. I discovered a man of great spiritual depth, deeply rooted in scripture, with a life centred on Christ and yet his feet firmly on the ground. Here was a man who, although he lived four and a half centuries before me, could put words to my experiences and offer words of wisdom for the journey. This connection with John's poetry and teachings not only helped to hydrate my soul during that dry spell but has also encouraged and sustained me to the present day. In fact, my current role as chaplain to Los Olivos, an ecumenical retreat centre in southern Spain, has been greatly influenced by Juan de la Cruz.

This book is about spiritual formation as a means to spiritual transformation. The chapters that follow will introduce you to the life of John of the Cross as well as his teachings and spiritual wisdom. Each chapter is an invitation to reflect on an aspect of the spiritual journey that John considered crucial if we are serious about our spiritual growth. It is also an invitation to prayer and to action, as you sit at the feet of the mystic who constantly points us to Christ, the Beloved. So, at the end of each chapter, you will have the opportunity to pray and reflect on John's teachings, often with reference to his poems. Most of John's poems can be found at the end of the book, with my own English translations opposite them.

There are at least two ways you can read this book. It can be an introduction to the key themes and spiritual teachings of John of the Cross. If that is what you are interested in, I hope you find these pages stimulating and that by the end of the book you will feel you know John and his God better. Alternatively, it can be a guide to spiritual formation, which you can follow as an individual or as part of a small group study. If you approach this book from the spiritual formation angle, I would encourage you to read it slowly, no more than one chapter each week, and to ensure that you are accompanied by a mentor or spiritual director in the process.

The content of this book is primarily the result of years of reading and praying through John's writings, but it is also the result of wonderful conversations with wise people who know Juan de la Cruz much better than I will ever do. In this respect, I am indebted to Colin Thompson, Antonio Ángel Aguilera OCD, and the various retreatants who have taken part in retreats on John of the Cross offered at Los Olivos. I am also deeply grateful to all those family and friends who have read the initial draft of this book, and have offered their invaluable suggestions and ongoing encouragement in the process. I would especially like to thank Guy Wynter, Andrew and Billie Tweedy and Naomi Starkey.

A great part of the material found in the following pages is an adaptation of the work I did, leading retreats on the poetry and spirituality of the Spanish mystic between 2010 and 2012. My prayer is that the following will enable you to grow deeper in your love for the Beloved and to become more like him.

Soli Deo Gloria.

Contents

Foreword

I was at a training event recently where we were all asked to think about the time in our lives when we had grown the most. For some reason I immediately found myself thinking of the first nine months of my life—the time I was growing in my mother's womb, the time I don't remember, but, without question, the time of my most radical growth. This in turn got me thinking about other things that happen without our effort or will. I grew in my mother's womb in darkness and unknowing. I grew because I was in the right environment. In the right place and at the right time, I was nurtured, fed, sustained and enabled. I was in a place where those dividing cells that were my first being could become what they were meant to be. I was beloved, and in the silence and darkness of the womb I grew.

These themes of our belovedness, of darkness, presence and unknowing are the stuff of the poetry and mystical theology of St John of the Cross, and they are offered to us here in this wonderful book through the meditations and lived-out spirituality of Daniel Muñoz. Here we can encounter the gentle, transformative power of St John's verse and vision.

I first met Daniel Muñoz in about 2008. He told me his dream of opening a retreat house in the beautiful mountains of the Sierra Nevada, close to Granada. Four years later I had the great joy of leading a retreat at *Los Olivos*, the house that he and Guy Wynter have opened. It is a place of beauty, warmth, stillness and wonderful hospitality. But although I was there to lead a retreat, there were, thankfully, moments in between when I could walk and think, pray and dream. There was also a lovely little library of books, quite a number either about St John of the Cross or anthologies of his verse. I knew about St John; I knew about his theology and poetry but, with one exception, I had never actually read the poems.

I also knew that St John had written a lot of other theological works, but I discovered that in the main they are really just profound meditations on the poems. It is the poems themselves that are at the heart of his spiritual vision, leading us deeper into the beauty of God, where the darkness of unknowing is realised as the greatest light of all—a blinding, dazzling darkness.

Therefore they are love poems, and when we first read them it would be easy to assume they are just about human love and desire. Of course they can be read this way, but, like the Song of Songs in the Bible, these poems are love songs to God, and beautiful echoes of God's love song to us in Jesus Christ.

So that week, in between the sessions I was leading, I immersed myself in the poems and found there the beauty and warmth of St John's rich and brilliant vision. Even 'vision' feels like the wrong word. St John doesn't show us something we might aspire to; rather, he leads us, often by the way of darkness, to a relationship of sumptuous love where we know ourselves to be the beloved and God the great and gracious lover.

The beauty and warmth of the poems was mirrored in the hospitality that Daniel was providing in the house and that was all around me in the austere splendour of the Spanish mountains.

As Daniel points out in the book, St John never teaches us how to pray. What he offers is an invitation to have everything else stripped back and to know God, to know that we are God's beloved; and to know that even in the hardest darkness of our lives, God can be encountered, that he is searching us out. This is a fountain whose 'clarity can never be obscured' and 'all light from it shines, although by night'.

+ *Stephen Cottrell, Bishop of Chelmsford*

Chapter 1

Life: The mystic and the poet

The qualities of the solitary bird are five: first, that it seeks the heights; second, that it admits of no companionship, not even with its own kind; third, that it stretches out its beak into the air; fourth, that it has no fixed colour; fifth, that it sings sweetly. These are the qualities that the contemplative soul has to possess... It has to sing sweetly for the love of its Spouse.[1]

These words by John of the Cross sum up his entire life—who he was and who he dreamt of being. St John of the Cross (in Spanish San Juan de la Cruz, or San Juan for short) is Spain's most universally appreciated Christian writer. His poems and works have been translated into many languages and have inspired people of all faiths to search for God in deeper and more meaningful ways.

John lived in Spain in the 16th century, at a time of unprecedented change and great challenges. The country had recently been unified by the Catholic monarchs Isabel and Ferdinand, with their conquest of Granada, the last Muslim kingdom in the Iberian peninsula. In the same year, 1492, Christopher Columbus had discovered the American continent in an expedition sponsored by the Spanish monarchs. The vision of king and queen was one of unity—political, linguistic and religious unity. The latter emphasis became the cause of much pain and heartache for many

Spaniards, but also the source of creativity and spiritual renewal.

For this religious unity to work, people of other faiths, principally Muslims and Jews, had to convert to Catholic Christianity. Since the alternative was to leave the country, most of them were baptised and became nominal Catholics. Despite the change of religious allegiance, however, the overall majority continued to practise their former faiths. The Holy Inquisition was established by the Catholic monarchs in Spain in 1478, as a religious police body that would make sure all new converts had fully and truly embraced the Catholic faith. Inquisition courts were set up all over the country and the so-called 'new Christians' became targets of close scrutiny.

Eventually, and following the example of most European nations, by the end of the 15th century all Jews had been expelled from the country, in one of the saddest episodes in Spanish history. Most became exiles in North Africa, while others moved to the eastern Mediterranean. (Some of these communities still preserve the culture, music and language of 15th-century Spain.)[2] A century later, following a series of military revolts in some villages south of Granada, the Muslim communities were also forced to leave their homes, livelihood and country of 700 years, and became refugees in North Africa.

Religious unity also meant that no dissent was allowed from within the Catholic population. Those who embraced the Protestant ideas that came from central Europe—mainly priests and monks who had read Martin Luther's works— also had to flee to safer havens in Europe. Those who tried to stay and form emerging Protestant communities in the country soon met with opposition from the Inquisition. A church reformation like the one taking place in central and northern Europe was avidly suppressed by monarchy and ecclesiastical authorities, for the sake of maintaining religious unity. Those Catholics who believed that a different type of Christianity was possible had only one way to change things—reforming their own church from within.

Many religious orders initiated a process of reform that modernised their institutions, in some cases made them more democratic and attempted to be more faithful to the evangelical[3] spirit of their founders. Some of these Catholic reformers went beyond superficial changes and sought a renewal of the spiritual life of their own communities, with an emphasis on contemplative prayer. This is the context in which John of the Cross lived and worked.

The early years

John was born in 1542 into a humble home in the village of Fontíveros, central Spain. He was the youngest of three brothers. His father died shortly after John was born and left his widow in a very difficult financial situation. Eventually, the family moved to the more prosperous town of Medina del Campo when John was nine.

John spent his formative years (1551–64) in Medina del Campo. During this period he developed a special interest in Christian spirituality, becoming increasingly involved in his local parish church. He worked as a volunteer at the local hospice, serving those who were terminally ill and raising funds for their care. He also devoted himself to the study of the arts at the Jesuit Colegio de la Doctrina, a boarding school for poor and orphaned children.

When he had completed his education, John joined the

Carmelite convent in Medina and, a year later, in 1564, he was sent to Salamanca to read Philosophy and Theology. At the time, the University of Salamanca was the most prestigious academic centre in Spain and one of the best in Europe. John's formation lasted four years, a time during which he received classic scholastic training and excelled as a student.

The Carmelite reform

The young friar was ordained priest in 1567. The year marked a turning point in John's life. That same summer, on a visit to Medina del Campo, he met Teresa of Ávila, a charismatic nun who had initiated a reform movement within the Carmelite order. Her objective was to form Christian communities that took seriously what she and others regarded as the radical call of the gospel—simplicity of living, serving God by serving others, and deep transformational prayer. At the time, John was experiencing a growing sense of discontent with the Carmelites and had been considering changing to a different religious order that placed more emphasis on contemplative prayer. Teresa shared with him her vision of reforming the order and creating new communities throughout the country, and John accepted the challenge to join her in this venture.

The following year, Brother Juan and two other friars became the first male reformers of the Carmelite order. Over the coming years, he established several community houses in Castille, central Spain, and got involved in some of the larger convents, including that of Segovia. In addition to building and restoring houses and leading some of these communities, John acted as mentor of novices and as *confesor* (spiritual director) to many nuns, including Teresa herself.

The reform, however, was not straightforward and it met

with the opposition of those who, within the order, did not want the sort of change that Teresa and John were promoting. 2 December 1577 became another turning point in Juan's life. That night, a group of unreformed friars broke into his community house in Ávila, kidnapped John and took him to the city of Toledo. There, he was tried and accused of being a rebel. The accusations were really based on some disputes and jurisdictional conflicts between the reformed and unreformed Carmelites.

In Toledo, John remained locked up for nine long months in a dingy cell, formerly used as a latrine. The cell was dark and cold, with virtually no ventilation. John was totally isolated, both physically and spiritually, from the outside world. In the midst of these inhumane conditions, which tested his physical, emotional and spiritual strength, the most wonderful poetry came to birth. First, without pen or paper, the friar sculpted in his memory and matured in his heart verses that expressed his spiritual journey and experience. Later, when he gained the favour of his jailer and was given pen and paper, he began to write down his verses in ink. So, in the blackness of his cell and out of the dark night of the soul that he experienced during his imprisonment, John wrote some of his best-known poems.[4]

Andalucía: freedom and fruitfulness

In August 1578, John escaped from his torment in Toledo. He had befriended the jailer, who gave him enough sheets to create a long rope. One night, the guard left his cell door unlocked, and John used a window on the wall of the house that led to the river, to climb down the wall and get to the path by the river. He then walked to the reformed Carmelite convent in the city and was looked after by the nuns until it became unsafe for him to stay there. With the support of these nuns he left for Andalucía, the southernmost region of Spain.

In this recently conquered land, the last bastion of Moorish rule in the Iberian peninsula, now repopulated with Christians who had moved from central and northern Spain, John regained his freedom and began a period of spiritual fruitfulness. He helped to found new community houses in the province of Jaen and eventually moved to the city of Granada, where he became the prior, or leader, of its reformed Carmelite convent.

Granada has been called the '*escritorio de San Juan de la Cruz*' ('Saint John of the Cross's writing desk'), for in these years of relative calm he was able to write more poems and most of his spiritual commentaries. In Granada, he continued to flourish as a mentor to young novices and as a spiritual director to older friars and nuns who were eager to draw closer to God.

During the latter years of John's life, he found himself immersed in new internal controversies with those who had different visions of the focus of reform. In 1590, these political tensions led him to fall out with the new leader who was heading the reform in Spain, Father Doria. The following year, at their General Chapter meeting in Madrid, the reformed Carmelites decided to send John to Mexico as a punishment—but that journey would never take place.

At the end of the summer of 1591, John became increasingly unwell and was taken to the convent in Úbeda (Jaén). The next few months would be a great test of personal endurance for the fragile priest. As he approached the end of his life, he had to suffer not only the pain of a terminal illness but also the inhumane treatment of Father Crisóstomo, the prior of the convent. John was allocated the worst cell in the house and kept in isolation from the rest of the friars who wanted to keep him company, following the prior's command. He was poorly fed and treated in the most unhygienic ways, dirty bandages being used while his body was increasingly covered by more and more tumours and ulcers. John's body gave up on 14 December. Towards the end, on his deathbed, he asked one of the friars standing by to read some verses from Song of Songs, his favourite book of the Bible. He was now ready for his final journey, to be warmly embraced by his God, fully transformed by the Beloved.

The mystic and the poet

Nowadays, John of the Cross is regarded by many primarily as a great poet and writer. In fact, he is still considered by many scholars as the finest poet of Spanish Golden Age literature (16th–17th centuries). Many books have been written providing helpful literary and linguistic studies of his poetry, shedding light on the intricate meaning of some of his most obscure texts.

However, John's poetry, as we have already seen, was a channel that pointed to a higher and deeper reality—that of God's work and presence in his life. In this sense, his poetry expresses a living faith and a spiritual journey—one that at times is full of longing, because of an experience of God's absence, and at other times full of the most wonderful shouts of joy, out of a deep encounter with Christ. His poetry is born out of his mystical experience. John is a mystic first and a poet second.

Some people think of mystics, and, by extension, of John

of the Cross, as solitary people who live in a permanent state of spiritual ecstasy, praying in their cells and absorbed in deep contemplation, or levitating with their robes floating in the air. This was not John's experience, certainly not most of the time. He was a very ordinary man who faced many challenges in his life, got his hands dirty with manual labour and endured great hardship and physical and emotional pain.

John, in the tradition of all good monastic spirituality, found it impossible to separate his spiritual life from the more practical aspects of his existence. His was a holistic spirituality that impacted everything that he did and every aspect of his identity. So he was able to make compatible his love for nature with his love for God, and his role as a leader and reformer of the Carmelite order with his job of project-managing building restorations, building walls and landscaping gardens. All of these practical tasks reflected what God was doing in his life, restoring and landscaping his soul, and also what he, as a mentor and spiritual director, could encourage in the lives of the young novices who joined his community.

One of the most significant aspects of mystical spirituality, in John's context, was its accessibility to people of all backgrounds. At a time when the main emphasis was placed on intellectual spirituality (you had to be a learned person to understand the things of God), John and Teresa modelled a new kind of spirituality, rooted in an experiential, prayerful and sacramental life. Anyone who was serious enough about their walk with God could experience God's reality, his love and his power.[5]

This was the path of spiritual formation chosen by John, one that focused on having a deeper, more experiential, ultimately transformational relationship with God. The mystics believed that the God in whom 'we live and move and have our being', to quote Paul's words to the people of Athens (Acts 17:28), can be found deep within us. The journey that San Juan invites us to follow is an inner journey, through which we become more aware of who we are and more aware of who God is. This is a journey of discovery and transformation, in which we become more and more the person we were created to be, achieving our full human potential, as we set our eyes above, on Christ, yet keep our feet on the ground.

For prayer and reflection

Reflect on your own life journey. You may find it helpful to draw a timeline on paper and identify some of the big turning points in your life. These could be changes or transitions connected with moving school, moving home, or experiencing a positive or negative event in your life.

These turning points are part of your story, and many of them will have helped to shape you into the person you are. Take some time to offer them to God in prayer.

You may also find it helpful to think of two or three individuals who have had a positive impact on your life. How did they touch your life? What did you learn from them? Take some time to thank God for their lives and for what they mean or meant to you.

Chapter 2

Night: The road less travelled

'Enter through the narrow gate. For wide is the gate and broad is the road that leads to destruction, and many enter through it. But small is the gate and narrow the road that leads to life, and only a few find it.'
MATTHEW 7:13–14

It is said of Juan de la Cruz that one day, as he travelled on foot through the plain fields of Castille with another friar, Juan de Jesús María, looking at the tall grass around them, he stopped and said to his companion, 'Let us continue our journey on this path that has not been trodden, for no one who has offended God has ever walked on this grass.'[6]

Robert Frost wrote a famous poem, 'The road not taken', in which he describes making a choice between two pathways in a wood: like John of the Cross, he decided to take the grassier path that 'wanted wear'.[7] At the heart of John's understanding and experience of the Christian journey is the choice, whenever possible, to walk on the road less travelled. This is not a capricious choice but, rather, one rooted in the teachings of the Rabbi of Nazareth, who advised his followers to look for the narrow gate and the road that few find.

When it comes to the many choices we face along our journey of faith, there is one that stands at the centre of all. For John, this is deeply connected with an experience that he describes as 'night' and has come to be known as the 'dark night of the soul'.

You may wonder why we should start to map out John's spirituality by talking about darkness and night. Surely there must be more positive images, more uplifting ideas in the teachings of the mystic that we could start with. It is true that the poet uses manifold pictures to describe the spiritual journey. However, if we are truly to understand John's vision of the journey of the human soul to God, we cannot do so without reference to his overarching metaphor—the night.

The Welsh Carmelite author Iain Matthew, in his book *The Impact of God*, sets the symbol of night in the context of John's life. First, in a general way, he reminds us of John's 'fascination for night-time which seems to have run in the family. His brother Francisco would sometimes be found outside in the fields late at night, lying beneath the starlit Castilian sky, arms stretched out in the form of a cross. So, long after dark, the friars would come across John outside near the trees praying, or he would be leaning at his window looking into the dark.'[8] Second, Matthew roots John's coinage of 'night' as a spiritual symbol in his experience of imprisonment in Toledo, where he escaped at night and found his freedom in the night.[9]

Perhaps this explains why, for John, the night is not a negative but a positive image that informs and shapes our spiritual journey and leads to spiritual transformation. In one of his best-known poems, *La Noche Oscura* ('The dark night'), he begins by affirming that the journey that leads to an intimate encounter with Christ the Beloved (*El Amado*) begins and takes place in the night.

On a dark night,
on fire with love's deepest yearnings,
oh, blessed chance,
unnoticed I left my home,
my house being now all stilled. (Night, *verse 1*)

Later in the same poem, he describes the night as 'blessed' or 'happy' (*dichosa*), for in the night the soul is able to journey, guided by the light of God in the heart.

In that blessed night,
in secret, for no one saw me,
I did not look around,
with any other light or guide,
save the one that burned within my heart. (Night, *verse 3*)

Finally, the night, which is described as 'more gentle than the dawn' (*noche amable más que el alborada*), becomes the backdrop for the transforming encounter with the Beloved. This encounter changes all things:

Oh, night that guided me,
oh, night more gentle than the dawn,
oh, night that united
Beloved and loved one,
loved one transformed in the Beloved!

The night, therefore, marks the beginning of the journey; it is the place where God is sought and found, and the locus where we can experience intimacy with Christ as Beloved. The night, for John, has a transformational power and a redemptive power.[10] These are some of the positive aspects of the night.

On one level, the night describes a universal human experience, shared by all people, when at different times in our lives we experience pain, loss, difficulties and challenges. We might argue that these are the 'nights' that choose us— nights over which we have no control. The key thing, then, is how we respond to these nights, whether with hopelessness and defeat or with the eyes of faith, putting our trust in the God who can be found in the night.

The four nights

Classic mystical tradition saw the earthly journey of the human soul to union with God as taking three stages. The first was the purgative path (*via purgativa*), in which the soul had to purge itself from all the baggage that hindered union with God. The second was known as the illuminative way (*via iluminativa*), in which the soul experienced glimpses of God's presence and a new light, or understanding. The third stage was the unitive path (*via unitiva*), in which full union with God was achieved and the soul was transformed into the likeness of God. So, for San Juan, the night becomes the backdrop of the mystic journey that involves inner purging, spiritual enlightenment and final union with God. It also becomes a symbol both of our free and deliberate choice to walk on the road less travelled and of what God does in us and through us through that process.

John of the Cross divides the human quest for a transforming intimacy with God into four moments, or stages, or seasons. These are distinctive 'nights' in which the spiritual focus is on particular aspects of our lives.

The first two nights refer to what *we* do in our spiritual journey to draw closer to God and be united to the Beloved.

John calls these the 'active' nights, because in them we actively seek intimacy with God through some serious inner work. These seasons involve practising life-giving spiritual disciplines that seek detachment from external things, so that we can focus wholeheartedly on God. They are nights that we choose to enter as we leave our 'home', all that is familiar and comfortable, and travel in search for God through uncharted territory. The journey is not an easy one, for it takes us out of our comfort zones and can lead to inner struggle and pain. It is experienced as a dark night in which faith is the only guide.

These two active nights are known as the 'active night of the senses' (in other words, one that focuses on external things, aiming to declutter our souls from all that is not of God in our lives) and the 'active night of the spirit' (that is, one that focuses on our inner world, on more subtle internal issues that act as blockages in the journey).

The other two nights refer to what *God* does in us, through the Holy Spirit, to prepare our hearts and souls for the gift of intimacy and union. These nights are called 'passive' because in them we are no longer in control; they are God's work from beginning to end. One of these seasons is the 'passive night of the senses': in other words, it is about what God does in us to help us see (touch, feel or hear) the world in the way that he sees (touches, feels or hears) it. Then there is the 'passive night of the spirit', also known as the final stage of the journey. Here, the focus is on what God does in us, by his grace, to purify our soul in its deepest centre, so that we can experience true intimacy with God in its purest form.

The passive night of the spirit is, by far, the most important and the toughest night of all, for here we experience utter nakedness before God. The things that we thought we knew about God are no longer relevant or useful, and we find ourselves in the dark, knowing that we know nothing (or very little really) about this God who calls us to intimacy. It can be felt as a time of absence, when God is nowhere to be found and our experience of God is of someone who is hiding. This is echoed in the opening words of John's poem *Spiritual Canticle*:

> *Where did you hide,*
> *Beloved, and left me crying?*
> *You fled like the stag,*
> *having wounded me.*
> *I left searching for you, and you were gone.*
> (Spiritual Canticle, *verse 1*)

This experience is shared by many women and men of God, at some point along the journey, and it helps us identify and connect with Christ's cry of abandonment on the cross: 'My God, my God, why have you forsaken me?' (Matthew 27:46). One of the most recent Christian public figures to have described it is Mother Teresa of Calcutta. Many were shocked to read in her diary that for many years, she lived her very own dark night of the soul, in which her experience of God was that of absence. Throughout that long season of her life, the only thing that kept her going was her ministry of service among the poor, and the only place where she saw God present was in the very people to whom she ministered.[11]

In the night, however, it is not only absence that is experienced; we can also experience presence. The movement described in John's poems, especially *Night* and *Canticle*, is from absence to presence, from a feeling of abandonment to one of fulfilment. In fact, it is only because the night ultimately becomes the place where God is profoundly present that our encounter with God in the night has a transforming power.

Knowing and unknowing

Two opposing, contrasting images are also associated with the night—knowing and unknowing. For John, we have to live with them both in the journey, and we have to learn to hold them together in creative tension. This is wonderfully described by the mystic in his poem, 'I entered where I knew not', which says:

Those who truly reach this place,
They now die unto themselves.
All they understood before,
Seems to them, too low a knowledge,
And His knowledge growing in them,
Means they remain there unknowing,
All knowledge transcending. (Verse 4)

Based on this poem, we might say that the night can be experienced also as a period of unlearning, in order for us to know afresh who is the God who calls us to intimacy. In that process of unlearning, the things that we thought we knew about God are put to the test. Questions arise, doubts emerge and, all of a sudden, old certainties appear to be less certain. The spiritual practices that used to 'work' in the past, in our prayer life, Bible meditations and Sunday worship, do not seem to 'do it' any more, and we need to discover new ways of connecting with God that are meaningful and life-giving.

This unlearning in order to learn new things is an invitation to conversion, again and again. It is also an invitation to be real about where we are in our journey with God and about the questions and doubts along the way. In the night we are given permission to ask questions, to live with uncertainties, to wrestle with paradoxes and to encounter and know God, 'all knowledge transcending'.

Yet the night is also a place where God is known. In his poem *Fonte* (*Fountain*), John uses a series of images to describe what God is like and the fact that he knows this God, although it is night (*aunque es de noche*). 'Night' is mentioned twelve times in the eleven verses, and ten times he uses the verb 'to know'. Oxford scholar and author of *Songs in the Night*, Colin Thompson, says that in order to understand this poem, we need to be familiar with the symbolism of John's Gospel—especially the encounter between Jesus and Nicodemus in the night (ch. 3) and the encounter between Jesus and the Samaritan woman by the well (ch. 4).

The two metaphors of water and darkness are used by the Gospel writer to describe God's life and life on this earth, respectively. John of the Cross draws from these two symbols in a free and creative way. The only point at which he departs from the Gospel writer in the meaning of the images is when it comes to darkness. While the Beloved Disciple uses the metaphor of darkness in a negative way (see John 1:5; 3:2; 13:30b), for the poet, darkness and night are places of new possibilities—the greatest of all being the possibility of encountering the Beloved. In this respect, and in line with Christian mystic tradition, 'darkness becomes a form of light, a locus of revelation'.[12]

The truths that John explores in *Fonte*, 'although by night', are connected with both faith and experience. By faith, he knows that 'the fountain that springs and flows' (God the Trinity) is the source of all life ('all origin from it derives').

He knows that this God is eternal and infinite ('there is no ending to this fountain' and 'no one may traverse its waters'). Also, as a Catholic priest, by faith he knows that this God is present 'within this living bread to give us life', in a clear allusion to the Eucharist. Alongside these almost credal affirmations, John knows by experience that God's 'flooding current is so mighty', and he knows 'of its power and its force'. He also knows that when the faithful are gathered around God's table, 'here they drink and have their fill, because it is night'. So, faith and experience inform our knowledge (albeit limited) of God on this earth.

In John's writings we see that both the experience of absence and that of unknowing/knowing in the night are part and parcel of the process of spiritual growth. Once God, through the Holy Spirit, has drawn close to us and we have experienced a deepening of our relationship with God, and once this relationship is established, God wants us to continue growing. It is that transition to an ever deeper relationship with God that leads to a new moment of crisis, to another night of the soul.

Night and spiritual growth

Of the many dimensions locked up in the symbol of night, 'growth' stands at its core. The night is the place where growth happens, where God stretches our spiritual muscles, where we experience maturity and increasingly reach our full potential as human beings. This does not mean that spiritual growth cannot take place in other ways. It certainly can. However, in the same way that certain life crises make us stronger, the experience of night can shape us spiritually more and more into the likeness of Christ.

John uses a wonderful picture to describe this process of maturity through the night. Drawing from the mother–child relationship, he writes:

> God nurtures and caresses the soul, after it has been resolutely converted to his service, like a loving mother who warms her child with the heat of her bosom, nurses it with good milk and tender food, and carries and caresses it in her arms. But as the child grows older, the mother withholds her caresses and hides her tender love; she rubs bitter aloes on her sweet breast and sets the child down from her arms, letting it walk on its own feet so that it may put aside the habits of childhood and grow accustomed to greater and more important things. The grace of God acts just as a loving mother by re-engendering in the soul new enthusiasm and fervour in the service of God. With no effort on the soul's part, this grace causes it to taste sweet and delectable milk and to experience intense satisfaction in the performance of spiritual exercises, because God is handing the breast of his tender love to the soul, just as if it were a delicate child.[13]

This image from developmental human psychology could be used to describe the process and stages of human maturity on other levels (social, relational or educational). For John, this image speaks powerfully about who God is and how God works in the passive night.

Later in the same commentary, John echoes the words of Jesus in Luke 15:7, 'there will be more rejoicing in heaven over one sinner who repents…', to describe the heavenly celebrations over those who grow spiritually in the night.

There is rejoicing in heaven that God has now taken
from this soul its swaddling clothes; that he has put it
down from his arms and is making it walk alone; that he
is weaning it from the delicate and sweet food of infants
and making it eat bread with crust; and that the soul is
beginning to taste the food of the strong (the infused
contemplation of which we have spoken), which in these
sensory aridities and darknesses is given to the spirit that is
dry and empty of the satisfactions of sense.[14]

Spiritual formation, therefore, says the Spanish mystic, is
about spiritual transformation. It is about growth, movement
and change. (Some of these aspects will be explored in our
next chapter.) In Colin Thompson's words, 'One of San
Juan's most important contributions to the history of Christian spirituality is to give a necessary and positive value
to experiences of inner frustration and paralysis. Like the
dark nights themselves, they have to be faced, but rightly
understood and used they become a means of growth.'[15]

The road less travelled

The notion of night, and of the moments or stages described
by the mystic, is neither prescriptive nor chronological.
John does not say that the only way to experience spiritual
growth is by going through seasons of night. He teaches
that periods of night can become moments of growth to
spiritual maturity. Likewise, although in his commentaries he
attempts to make a systematic exposition of the four stages
as a linear experience, we see that in his own life this was
not the case. John himself experienced seasons of night, of
sequedad (spiritual dryness) and of absence of God after he

had enjoyed moments of deep intimacy and union with the Beloved.

The night, as the overarching metaphor in John's understanding of the spiritual journey, is both the way of self-denial at the heart of the gospel and the way of love which was incarnated by the Beloved. It is our response to Christ's invitation to deny our self-centred nature in order to follow him (Matthew 16:24), as well as Christ's promise to give us fullness of life on this earth (John 10:10). It is our conscious affirmation to serve one rather than two masters (Matthew 6:24), knowing that God will provide for all our needs (Matthew 6:33). It is our deliberate choice to enter through the gate that leads to the road less travelled, in order to discover what God can do in us and through us in that journey. This is what the night, for John, stands for.

For prayer and reflection

Read the stories of Jesus' conversations with Nicodemus and the Samaritan woman in John 3 and 4. Reflect on these two encounters, especially on the symbol of night as the backdrop of the dialogue with Nicodemus, and water in the discussion with the woman at the well.

Then read the poem *Fountain* as a prayer, reflecting on the symbol of God's living water in your life, especially at times when you have been particularly aware of the night.

Chapter 3

Movement: The Christian journey

'If I take one more step, it will be the furthest away from home I've ever been.'[16]

In the spring of 2011 we ran our first St John of the Cross retreat at Los Olivos. The retreat was an introduction to the Carmelite friar's teachings, both through an exploration of his poems and through flamenco music and dance. The first session was entitled 'Movement' and had two parts. In the morning we studied together the poem *Dark Night*, its symbolism, metaphors and spiritual wisdom. In the afternoon we had a flamenco workshop in which Carmen Álvarez, a professional flamenco dancer and choreographer, introduced us to some of the key movements and rhythms of this ancient form of dance. The new movements we were invited to explore with our bodies reflected the deeper movements we had been invited to embark on in our souls—movements that John depicts at the beginning of *Night* with the following words:

> *On a dark night,*
> *on fire with love's deepest yearnings,*
> *oh, blessed chance,*
> *unnoticed I left my home,*
> *my house being now all stilled. (Verse 1)*

The picture John gives us in this poem is a familiar one. It is the experience of the person who, having waited with anticipation for a well-deserved holiday at a wonderful place in the sun, tidies up at work and at home, packs her bags, locks her house and gets on a plane for a special journey. Or the experience of the lover who, having lived away from his loved one for a long time, rethinks the priorities in his life, books some time off work, organises his desk and his house and travels a long way to meet his loved one.

The opening words of the poem evoke movement as a positive thing—in fact, as an essential part of life. Colin Thompson sees the two poems *Night* and *Spiritual Canticle* as having this positive notion of movement in common. He writes, 'Like the "Noche" but on a wider scale, the apparently fragmented narrative and language of the poem [Canticle] represent the movement from separation to union. But that movement is not something the critic imposes from without. It is inherent in the way San Juan handles language.'[17] Movement in John's poetry, then, is not just an image associated with specific verbs (such as 'left',[18] 'entered',[19] 'fled', 'climb', 'walk' and 'flying'[20]). Rather, he uses the overall flow and rhythm of each poem, often jumping from moment to moment, from scene to scene, to give the reader the sensation of movement.

The idea of movement in *Night* is also full of mystery and secrecy. The journey begins:

In darkness and secure,
down the secret ladder, disguised…
in darkness and concealment,
my house being now all stilled. (Verse 2)

This movement takes place in the night, on the road less travelled, full of mystery and unknown things. It is a movement that stops only when the loved one finds the Beloved, 'in a place where no one appeared' (verse 4), with no witnesses around. That is the end of the journey—the encounter with the Beloved, which will be explored in more detail in Chapter 7 when we look at 'transformation'—but what is the beginning of the journey?

The starting point of the movement is the house or home (*mi casa*). The house, in the poem, is a metaphor for the soul and all the domestic activities that distract us or keep us busy—the noise in our lives that absorbs us, tires us and feeds our ego, our self-centred nature. In his commentary on the poem *Night*, John observes:

> It was a sheer grace for this soul that God in this night puts
> to sleep all the domestic members of its household, that is,
> all the faculties, passions, affections, and appetites that live
> in the sensing soul [our human nature] and that prevent
> the soul from coming out of itself and of the house of the
> senses, to the perfect spiritual union of God's perfect love.[21]

The above categories, namely faculties, passions, affections and appetites, which are based on medieval scholastic distinctions, should not confuse or distract us. John's language here, as in all his commentaries, is a product of its time and would have been understood by those who read it. The important thing to remember here is that, in describing all the dimensions of the person known to him, John is concerned with the entire person. His is a holistic form of spirituality. The movement he advocates is one that involves the whole person, not just a part of who we are.

Decluttering the soul

At the beginning of the journey, John gives a lot of attention to a process that I call the 'decluttering' of the soul.[22] This is connected with the 'active night of the senses' explored in the previous chapter. It is a bit like moving house. With any house move, you have to go through everything you have accumulated through the years. You have to select what you want to keep and take to the new home, while being ruthless about getting rid of useless or unused things. The process will involve trips to the recycling centre or the local charity shops. It will also involve packing away the belongings that are important and precious to you, so that they can be carried safely to their new home.

The Spanish mystic affirms that, in personal spiritual formation and as part of the journey to spiritual transformation, we need to take time to identify and understand all the clutter in our souls. In some instances, it may be linked to attachments or desires—desire for success and affirmation; desire to avoid pain or confrontation; desire to fulfil our dreams and hopes. Many of these desires may be seen as 'normal' or, at the very least, as human. For Darwinists, they would be the result of our survival instinct, part of the process of natural selection. The 'self' seeks to survive in this violent, volatile and hostile world, if possible, with the least amount of suffering and pain. Many of our desires for safety and affirmation have their opposites in fears and anxieties (some irrational) about difficult or painful situations that may take us out of our comfort zone.

Developmental psychology has shown that many of the fears and anxieties that dwell in our minds have deep roots that go back to our childhood or even beyond (some are influenced by our genetic baggage). Some of them have a positive role: they protect us and help us survive by warning us about danger so that we can avoid it. Other fears, however, prevent us from growing as human beings. They paralyse us or make us hide or lead us to find excuses not to face them. These fears make us stay at home, locked in, surrounded by familiar things, preventing us from going out into unknown territory, away from our comfort zones. They cause us to avoid risks and turn our spiritual muscles stiff. Faith in the Beloved no longer means anything, for fear doesn't just paralyse; it can destroy faith altogether, first restricting faith to small things and later extinguishing it completely. Instead, we put our trust in our own ability to survive in the safe, comfortable and familiar space of our home.

Fear makes us choose stagnation rather than movement. It causes us to remain static instead of changing. John of the Cross knew well that the transforming power of the gospel can enable us to conquer fear. 'Do not fear' seems to be one of the most often-repeated commands in scripture from the mouth of God, and Jesus, as Bernhard Hanssler shrewdly observes, seems to be 'the only founder of a world religion who has removed the element of fear from religion'.[23]

Yet fear is not the only blockage that impedes us from leaving our 'home' behind in search for the Beloved. At the heart of this process of decluttering, San Juan places the notion of detachment or nakedness of all things. This does not mean that we have to get rid of all material possessions or emotional attachments but rather that we have to redefine our relationship with the objects (and people) around us. This idea is based on Jesus' teaching: 'No one can serve two masters; for a slave will either hate the one and love the other, or be devoted to the one and despise the other. You cannot serve God and wealth' (Matthew 6:24, NRSV).

For John, attachment to certain things and/or people, and to what they stand for, can be equally paralysing. In his commentaries, he deals with all sorts of areas of our lives in which our attachment to things, or relationships of unhealthy dependence on things or people, can get in the way of our spiritual growth. This is not just attachment to what John calls 'temporal' things, such as our house, our job, our car or people we are particularly fond of (children, our spouse, friends, a church leader or a spiritual director). It also refers to our desire for or enjoyment of certain attributes that we find in other people or in ourselves, whether 'natural' (such as beauty, grace, youth or understanding) or 'moral' (for example, virtue, acts of kindness or keeping God's law).[24] The danger is that, by having an unhealthy relationship with any of these, it can lead to 'vanity, pride, and vainglory'.[25]

Likewise, there are other areas in which we may experience a similar sense of attachment or desire. John labels these more subtle forms of attachment as 'supernatural' and 'spiritual'. They are connected with our enjoyment of, and attachment to, particular spiritual practices that make us 'feel good' but carry the risk of becoming an end in themselves rather than a means to an end—the end being God.[26] John devotes what seems like a disproportionate number of chapters in his commentaries to this subject. In the context of his primary readership—contemplative religious people, for whom these spiritual practices were part and parcel of life—it makes sense that John would spend time addressing these issues. But he also brings a warning to those of us who are not nuns or monks and yet consider ourselves disciples of the Teacher of Nazareth.

In all of the above, John invites us constantly to watch

our motivations and our relationships to all that is around us as we engage in the process of inner decluttering. San Juan encourages those who are serious about following Christ to reprioritise all their attachments and realign all their desires to one supreme goal—that of serving God. This becomes the test of all else. If my relationships to everything and everyone I count as dear are life-giving (in the sense that they enable me to come closer to God), they have to be nurtured. If they are not, then they need to be redefined, reworked and reoriented. Therein lies part of the movement.

The journey to freedom

There is a classic story in the book of Exodus that describes a journey. It is the story of Moses leading the people of Israel out of Egypt to the promised land, out of slavery into freedom, out of the old into the new. In that journey there was a lot of moving around, leaving behind and walking away, but deep down, in people's psyches, the moving had not really taken place. They continued to look back, to miss things, to feel like slaves. Someone once said that it was easy for God to get the Israelites out of Egypt but much harder to get Egypt out of the Israelites. There was a lot of decluttering to be done in their minds and hearts and souls.

San Juan does not say that this decluttering process, when taken seriously, is easy. Quite the opposite: he compares it to a dark night in which we are tested to our core and in which both fears and attachments have to be overcome so that we can get close to the Beloved. Through it, however, true inner freedom is found and we are able to achieve our full potential as human beings. The journey to freedom, as the people of Israel discovered, can take a long time. It can feel as if we are taking one step forward and two steps back—but, as the mystic says, if we persevere we will not be disappointed.

This journey, John teaches, demands a decision of faith and love. Faith is the antidote to fear: we trust that the Holy Spirit, God's 'living flame of love', will guide us to the Beloved. Faith is the light that guides the soul in the dark night and, according to John, 'burned within my heart'. Love is the antidote to desire. This is the drive that moves us towards God, 'on fire with love's deepest yearnings'. Love becomes the motivation for the journey and, at the same time, love is the destination. So, just as fears and desires are the two sides of a single coin, faith and love work together, leading and guiding us towards the Beloved.

The movement of the soul

At a recent leadership formation course, I was invited to speak at one of the sessions, which explored the notion of the contemplative (or mystic) as a leader. After sharing some of my thoughts on what makes a mystic leader distinctive, using primarily Juan de la Cruz and Teresa de Avila as my role models, someone in the group raised a very interesting question. He described his understanding of leadership as involving movement—that is, taking or leading a group of people from here, 'A', to there, 'B'. He went on to say that his understanding of the mystic was of someone who was interested not in movement but in stillness. For him, the contemplative was more concerned with being in the present (or Presence) than with doing things that involve change and movement (both of which are central to leadership). His conclusion was, therefore, that being a contemplative and being a leader was a contradiction in terms.

While I had to agree with the fundamental premises in this person's argument, regarding the primary roles of a leader and of a contemplative person, I could not share the final conclusion. A contemplative teacher like San Juan, as we have already seen, would be deeply interested in change and movement of the right kind. He believes that the important movement is the one taking place in our souls, which takes us from where we are to where God is. Perhaps this would be more accurately rephrased as a movement that takes us from how we are, here and now, to how we will be as we experience deep intimacy with God and become more like the Beloved. It is a qualitative movement that leads to a qualitative, rather than quantitative, change.

In one of his commentaries, San Juan explores this very issue. Discussing the notion of supernatural visions, he describes the movement of the soul when she 'awakes' to God and delights in new things.

How this movement takes place in the soul, since God is immovable, is a wonderful thing, for it seems to the soul that God indeed moves; yet he does not really move. For since it is the soul that is renewed and moved by God, so it might behold this supernatural sight, and since divine life is revealed to it with such newness, it seems to the soul that it is God who moves, and the cause assumes the name of the effect it produces. According to this effect, we can assert that God moves, as the Wise Man says: 'For wisdom is more movable than all movable things' [Wisdom 7:24]. And this is not because she moves, but because she is the principle and root of all movement. 'Remaining in herself the same', as he goes on to say, 'she renews all things' [Wisdom 7:27]. Thus what he wishes to say in this passage is that wisdom is more active than all active things. We then ought to say that in this movement it is the soul that is moved and awakened from the sleep of natural vision to supernatural vision.[27]

Here, the movement is a change of perception. We no longer 'see' things through the lenses of our 'natural' eyes—that is, our self-centred human nature. We begin to 'see' reality through the lenses of God. This, in turn, affects the way we relate to all that is around us, from our relationships with others to our jobs or commitments, and from our spirituality and faith to our relationship with nature and creation.

For prayer and reflection

Take time to reflect on your own journey and think about your 'house'—that is, your spiritual house, your soul. First, look back on your life and on some of the big transitions that you have been through, moments when you had to leave things behind in order to embrace the new. How did it feel at the time? What sort of change was it? Did you choose it or did it choose you? Where was God in that change? What did you learn in the process?

Second, take time to reflect on the changes that you are experiencing in your life now. Are they like anything you have experienced before? Looking at the metaphor of spiritual clutter, what sort of clutter do you have to get rid of in your life to travel more lightly towards the Beloved? What are the attachments and fears that are not allowing you to leave your home? What are the relationships you have to redefine in order to move away from whatever is not life-giving, so that you can focus on all that gives you life?

Now read the poem *Night* as a prayer and reflect on your

own journey to God and how you have moved/changed along
the way.

Chapter 4

Nakedness: The heart of Christian prayer

One day Jesus was praying in a certain place. When he finished, one of his disciples said to him, 'Lord, teach us to pray.'
LUKE 11:1

Over the last few years at Los Olivos, we have enjoyed many mountain walks with groups of guests to nearby villages. The Sierra Nevada mountains can be very hot in the summer, and the sun particularly strong in the middle of the day, so before we head off for a walk, we go through the checklist. 'Are you wearing comfortable shoes?' 'Did you bring a hat?' 'Have you put on sun protection cream?' And, most importantly, 'Are you carrying plenty of water for the journey?'

Most times, about an hour or so into the walk, we would realise that someone had forgotten to bring water with them. We could tell by the fact that they would start getting grumpy with everybody else. They would complain about the weather being too hot, the track being too steep, and people walking too fast. It is a very common experience that when we feel dehydrated we get grumpy.

John Pritchard, the Bishop of Oxford, shared a similar story during a talk on Christian spirituality, and made a very interesting connection with society in general. He observed that when you have a conversation about ordinary life issues, many people's response is to be grumpy. Some seem to spend the whole time complaining about something, whether it's the government, the church, young people, the traffic or the weather. Bishop John's view was that our society is so grumpy because it is dehydrated—lacking not physical but spiritual water. In other words, the reason for some people's constant whining and grumpiness is simply spiritual dehydration. Of course, this behaviour is not present just in wider society but also in the church. The very communities and environments that should be spiritually hydrated are, at times, as much in need of spiritual water as is the rest of society.

The Bible is full of examples where water is used as a metaphor or symbol of spiritual life. One of my favourites is the story (in John 4) of Jesus talking to the woman by the well, asking for a drink of water and then offering her water that will prevent her from ever being thirsty again, that will hydrate her body and her soul, giving her abundant life. At the end of the conversation, the woman is eager to drink of Jesus' water of life, and, as a response, she brings her whole village to Jesus so that they too can be spiritually hydrated.

During his time in Granada as prior of the Convent of the Martyrs, just outside the Alhambra citadel walls, one of John's responsibilities was to mentor novices. It is said that, occasionally, he would wake the young would-be friars while it was still dark and, rather than going into chapel for morning prayer, he would take them down the hill to the River Darro. There, he made them sit in silence, listening to the sound of water, and encouraged them to use that time for prayer and contemplation. Some people think that the aim of this exercise was to help them become aware of God's presence in creation. Others believe that John wanted them to reflect on their need for God's living water in their lives. Whatever his real motivation, it is clear that, for San

Juan, water was a powerful symbol of divine life and spiritual hydration.

In *Fonte*, a poem that we have already seen in Chapter 2, John uses the metaphor of water to depict the God of life. In the introductory verse, God is compared to a spring of water or fountain *que mane y corre* ('that runs and flows'). This spring has no beginning, yet it is the beginning of all that there is (verse 2). It is a fountain full of power and might, with a radically inclusive nature, watering 'hell and heaven, and humanity' (verses 6 and 7). Perhaps most significantly, it is a source of life that can be experienced here and now, even in the dark, *aunque es de noche*. This point of repetition in the poem, 'although by night', connects with John's experience of imprisonment in Toledo. *Fonte* was written as a result of the nine months that he lived in the darkness of a dingy cell, built into the city wall above cliffs that led to a river, whose flowing water the poet could hear every night.

The repetition of 'night' is also connected with John's overarching theme, explored in Chapter 2, of the dark night of the soul. He believed that we can experience God even when we go through difficult times, when we do not have it all together, do not have all the answers or do not possess as much faith as we wished we had. And the most powerful way we can experience and encounter God, for John, as it was for Jesus, is through prayer.

The naked prayer

Unlike the other great Carmelite mystic and author, Teresa of Avila, Juan de la Cruz never teaches 'how' to pray. He presents no technique or method to guide us in our prayer life. The reason for this is simple. John is writing to women and men of prayer who have chosen the contemplative life in community as a means of coming closer to God. These are people who know a lot about prayer techniques. They know the 'what' and the 'how', but they do need help with the 'why' and the 'what for'—in other words, the motivation and purpose of their prayer life. Here, John has a lot to say, and what he does is to describe his own experience of prayer and offer it to his readers.

In his *Sayings of Light and Love*, he writes, 'Seek in reading and you will find in *meditation*; knock in prayer and it will be opened to you in *contemplation*' (Saying 158, emphasis added). John sees two ways in which we can connect with God in prayer: meditation and contemplation.

The first, meditation, takes place in our minds and is a 'discursive act carried out through images, forms and figures, fabricated and imagined by the senses'.[28] In this form of prayer we connect with God through words, thoughts and ideas. An example would be the practice of Ignatian meditation, in which we are encouraged to enter into a biblical story by imagining ourselves as part of that story. Nowadays, the technique known as visualisation, inspired by this form of meditation, is widely used in psychoanalysis. This form of prayer is useful because it helps a person to go deeper in their relationship with God. However, it can also be dangerous, in the sense that it can become an end in itself rather than a means to an end—the end being an encounter with God.

San Juan devotes a lot of energy to warning his readers about some of the dangers of meditation, especially connected with the idea of 'attachment' in prayer. If we develop a relationship of dependence on (attachment to) mental images and visions of God, they can end up taking the place of the true God, who is ultimately invisible, in our lives. He quotes three biblical sources to make his case: John 1:18, where we are told that no one has ever seen God; Isaiah 64:4, where the prophet declares, 'From ages past no one has heard, no ear has perceived, no eye has seen any God besides you' (NRSV); and Exodus 33:20, where God tells Moses that he cannot see God's face, for no one can see the divine face and live.[29]

The mystic concedes that visual meditation can be a helpful tool for encountering God at a particular time in our journey of faith. However, he wants his readers to consider a higher form of prayer. In his own words, 'even if the remembrance of these visions really does stir up the soul to some contemplation and love of God, *pure faith* and *nakedness*, and darkness of all such things, will stir and elevate it much more'.[30]

The prayer that elevates us to a higher-deeper experience of God is, for the poet, contemplation, also known as the 'naked prayer'. In Colin Thompson's words, 'All that is required is a naked, loving attention directed towards God, naked because it is not clothed in words, ideas or images.'[31] In contemplation, we follow Jesus' teaching on prayer, in which he encourages the person to go into their room (their innermost being), shut the door behind them (lay aside all distractions and attachments) and pray in secret, undressing the soul before God (Matthew 6:6).

One of the greatest definitions of contemplation came from the address of Pope Paul VI at the closing gathering of the Second Vatican Council. He said:

He is real, He lives, a personal, provident God, infinitely good; and not only good in Himself, but also immeasurably good to us. He will be recognised as Our Creator, our truth, our happiness; so much so that the effort to look on Him, and to centre our heart in Him which we call contemplation, is the highest, the most perfect act of the spirit, the act which even today can and must be at the apex of all human activity.[32]

Needless to say, the sort of prayer advocated by John in contemplation is one that takes place in silence and therefore requires no images and no words. It has also been called 'centring prayer', because in it the goal is to centre our hearts and minds on God, who speaks with us through silence and whose voice we hear in silence. In one of his *Sayings of Light and Love*, San Juan writes, 'God spoke one Word, which was his Son, and this Word he always speaks in eternal silence, and in silence must it be heard by the soul' (Saying 21).

It is in *profundo silencio* ('profound silence') that the soul listens to what God speaks to her in contemplation.[33] This is not just silence in the sense of no external audible noise. John points to a deeper and more subtle form of silence, one that affects the inner noise that we hear in our minds. For us to enter into contemplation fully, those inner noises also need to be switched off. John believes that the main source of these noises is our memory—that is, our capacity to remember things of the past or things that are going on in our lives in the present. In this respect, he teaches, 'But in our case we close the memory to all things—from which distractions and evils arise—by rendering it silent and mute, and listening to God in silence with the hearing of the spirit, saying with the prophet: "Speak, Lord, for your servant is listening"' (1 Samuel 3:10).[34]

John's understanding of prayer as a primarily silent-naked exercise, where we unclothe our hearts and minds of external noise and distractions, to focus only on God, has a great impact on the way he views intercessory prayer. Here, he follows Jesus' teaching to his disciples to use only few words in prayer, for our heavenly Father knows our needs and he will provide (Matthew 6:7–8). For John, the shorter the prayer, the greater the impact. 'The short prayer pierces the heavens,' he says in one of his commentaries.[35] He also believes that in order to achieve the desires of our hearts, we need to embrace all of God's promises, which are already available here and now. In one of his most beautiful prayers, John, in conversation with his soul, urges her to own the big picture and vision of all that she is and has in Christ.

> Why do you delay things and wait, since from this very
> moment you can love God in your heart? Mine are the
> heavens and mine is the earth. Mine are the peoples, the
> just are mine and mine are the sinners; the angels are
> mine, and the Mother of God, and all things are mine.
> And God himself is mine and for me, because Christ is
> mine, and all for me. What do you ask, then, and seek,
> oh my soul? All of this is yours, and all is for you. Do not
> engage yourself in something less or be concerned with
> the crumbs that fall from your Father's table. Go forth, and
> exult in your Glory! Hide yourself in it, and rejoice, and
> you will receive the petitions of your hearts. (*Sayings of
> Light and Love* 26).

What a wonderful invitation for the follower of Christ, in the form of a prayer, to enlarge our vision of things earthly and heavenly and to transcend what is small in order to embrace God's greatest gift—Christ in us, the hope of glory. And what an affirming promise for those who go deep in their relationship with God, that as we abide and rejoice in God, we will achieve the desires of our hearts.

Praying with scripture

Scripture, too, played a very important role in John's prayer life. It is clear from his writings that San Juan had a deep knowledge of the Bible. He quoted it extensively in his commentaries, expressing at the beginning of most of them that their main source was *la autoridad de la Sagrada Escritura* ('the authority of Holy Scripture').[36] He taught and unpacked the meaning of scripture to his Carmelite brothers, who were amazed at his wisdom and ability to bring it to life.[37] He was often seen reading the scriptures in public places and was known for always carrying a Bible when he went on his long journeys throughout Spain and Portugal. One of the best-known examples of this habit is described in a story from 1585, when John visited Lisbon for a Carmelite chapter meeting. While other members of the chapter went to visit a nun who claimed to have miraculous powers, John, sceptical of the nun, chose instead to go to the seaside to read and meditate on the Bible. When asked by a fellow friar why he had done so, he answered that he had no time for self-promoting con artists, and turned to his Bible.[38]

Again, when it came to praying with the scriptures, San Juan did not teach a method or technique. Others, like Ignatius of Loyola or Teresa of Avila, had taught on this subject at some length. What we see in John is a love for scripture that became contagious for the people he met. In the poet, we discover a creative reading and prayerful rewriting of some parts of the Bible, which he not only translated into

Spanish (at a time when the Bible was only available in Latin) but also reinterpreted as an artist in two of his poems. The best known of these is *Spiritual Canticle* (already mentioned), broadly inspired by the Song of Songs. The least-known, yet equally creative and moving, is the *Romances on the Gospel*, in which the mystic recounts the story told at the beginning of Saint John's Gospel. (See page 123 in this book for a translation.) In both poems, *Canticle* and *Romances*, San Juan the artist works with San Juan the theologian to bring to life a biblical narrative in a wonderfully creative way.

From these poems and his commentaries we observe how John of the Cross engaged with scripture—not as a science book, where he expected to find answers to scientific questions, but as a sacred book that provides wisdom and guidance for the spiritual journey. We also see how John approached the Bible. This is succinctly put by Colin Thompson:

> [The Bible's] place in the Church and the way it has inspired art and literature derive from a sense of its oneness and uniqueness, its mystery and its revelation. San Juan treats scripture as a whole and ranges freely through it, finding points for meaningful comment where words and images recur or complement each other... That is how he knew and cherished it.[39]

The Bible was John's prayer book. It was always on his bedside table and, more importantly, in his heart and mind. Scripture was one of the key places where the poet entered into conversation with the Beloved, through prayer and reflection, in silence and contemplation.

Prayer as an act of love

If scripture is a prayer book, and nakedness and silence the inner condition for prayer, then 'love' is the drive and the means by which contemplative prayer becomes a life-giving spiritual exercise. In the same way that love is the motivation for life, love has to be the motivation for prayer; and because love is a universal human experience, there is a sense in which everyone is able to connect with God through contemplative prayer.

For John, only *el alma enamorada* ('the soul in-love-with-God')[40] is able to pray in contemplation, for only those who are in love can undress their soul before the Beloved, in order to experience true intimacy. A number of times, he uses the noun 'love' as a synonym of 'contemplation', and the expression 'solitary love' as a synonym of the 'contemplative life', almost interchangeably. In one of his commentaries, he writes:

> Hence, when a soul possesses something of this degree of solitary love great harm would be done to herself and to the Church if even for a short time she was expected to be occupied in exterior or active matters, even if they were of great import... In the end, we were all created for this end of love. So let those who are very active and think to gird the world with their preaching and exterior works note that they would benefit the Church and please God a great deal more if they spent only half the time being with God in prayer.[41]

We can sense John's frustration, not just with his colleagues (friars, priests and preachers) who neglect contemplative prayer because they are too busy putting the world right, but also with those within his order who continue to entrust him with responsibilities that take him away from a contemplative life. Even in John's days, those who followed the Way of Jesus struggled to get the balance right between doing and being, work and prayer. He believed that this balance always needs to be readdressed, our prayer lives watched and our spiritual lives nurtured.

For prayer and reflection

If prayer is the way we hydrate ourselves spiritually and drink from God's living water, what sort of prayer do you feel less or more comfortable with—spoken, silent, meditative, contemplative or liturgical?

John encourages us to pray continually, constantly addressing the balance between our work, leisure and prayer lives. How much or little do you pray? What gets in the way of making time to pray?

If you can, find a quiet space to sit or go for a walk. Take time to pray in silence, with scripture, with one of John's poems, or simply feeling the rhythm of your own breathing. Allow your heart and mind to centre on God in this time of prayer, and enjoy just being in God's presence.

Chapter 5

Encounter:
The God of intimacy

The human heart, made in the size of God, cannot be satisfied with less than God.
ALFONSO BALDEÓN [42]

For John of the Cross, the entire human journey, our whole life, has only one goal—the transforming encounter with the Beloved. Only such encounter can truly fulfil us and give meaning and purpose to who we are and what we do. It was this encounter that changed his life and, according to him, is able to change our lives too. Moreover, as we have already seen in Chapter 2, it has the power to change our perception of God (how we see him) and, ultimately, the way we relate to God and to the rest of the world.

The image we have of God is very important to San Juan. If you were to draw a picture of God or describe God in words or metaphors, what would God look like? If you were able to pick one piece of sacred art from a church or a museum that depicted God in some way, which would it be? We have all been exposed, from our childhood onward, to multiple images (not all graphic) of God. Maybe we see God as a long-bearded old man, looking down from the clouds with an angry face, ready to spoil our fun on earth. Perhaps we see him as a young man, hanging on a cross, helpless, powerless and unable to help us; or as a serious teacher, holding a book with one hand, giving a blessing with the other and looking intently at us in a somewhat disapproving way.

Jesus himself used stories to paint different pictures of God—as a running father (Luke 15:11–32), a rejoicing woman (vv. 8–9), a caring shepherd (Matthew 18:12–14), a hidden treasure or a precious pearl (Matthew 13:44–46).[43] So did San Juan. In his poetry, as we have seen already, God is depicted as a running fountain, a living flame of love, a hiding lover and a protective bridegroom. These are some of the best-known pictures of the divine that captured the imagination of the poet and expressed his encounters, but others will be explored below.

There is a lovely story of a conversation between John and Brother Francisco, known to be of innocent and simple faith, one day during the period of recreation in the convent in Granada. 'Tell us, Brother Francisco, what is God like?' asked John. The friar raised his hand, scratched his head and, after a little thought, replied, 'Reverend Father, God is whatever he wants to be.' Then John, recognising the depth of his brother's answer, talked at some length about God's independence, sovereignty, freedom and generosity toward us.[44]

Suppose we were to ask John that same question: 'Tell us, Brother John, who is your God? What does your God look like? In your experience, how would you describe God?' What would the mystic say? We shall explore some of his possible answers below.

God is the relentless 'seeker' of human beings

This may be a simple idea, but it is hugely profound and has important implications for the way we relate to God. We often think of ourselves as spiritual seekers. We are the ones who take the initiative to seek God. For John, however, there is no doubt that it is the other way round. He writes, 'In the first place it should be known that if anyone is seeking God, the Beloved is seeking that person much more.'[45]

In one of his best-known *Sayings of Light and Love*, he reaffirms this idea with great poetic passion: 'O Lord, my God, who will seek you with simple and pure love, and not find that you are all one can desire, for you show yourself first and go out to meet those who seek you?' (Saying 2). It is God who initiates the search, who takes the first step by coming out towards us, who is eager to meet us, to embrace us and to lavish his love on us.

The journey in the night, then, is not about us but about God. John, the spiritual teacher, does not provide us with an easy, ready-made self-help spiritual programme, aimed at boosting our ego and making us feel good about ourselves and the world. The path he sets before us is the radical path of Christian discipleship. His aim is to help us journey through the night to a life-changing encounter with God, where the Beloved touches and transforms our life in its deepest centre with his living flame of love. The journey is not about us but about God. In John's words, 'this is a venture in which God alone is sought and gained; thus only God ought to be sought and gained'.[46] God is the insatiable, relentless, passionate seeker of women and men.

In his *Romance on the Gospel*, San Juan makes this point clear with deeply evocative language. 'In the beginning' there was only God, the Trinity—'Three persons and one Beloved', in reference to Christ's special place within the loving community of God. Then, out of love, God takes the initiative to create the world and human beings, which he calls 'the

Bride'. Later, also out of love, God takes the initiative to come to us, to become human, in order to seek us and draw us back to intimacy with the Beloved. The poet describes that moment of God-becoming-human with emotive language:

> *The time had now arrived*
> *for the baby to be born...*
> *Men sang canticles divine,*
> *Angels melodies unknown...*
> *But God, in the manger,*
> *there, he wept and cried;*
> *These were the jewels that the bride*
> *brought to her wedding day.*
> *Whilst the mother, in amazement,*
> *watched this awesome exchange*
> *the weeping of man in God*
> *and in man the divine joy.* (Romances, *Part IX*)

It is God who, in Christ-the-Beloved, takes the initiative to seek us, and it is when our human search meets God's that we can experience the life-giving and life-changing encounter with the Beloved.

God as the 'exalter' of human beings

John believes God seeks us for one purpose alone—not intimacy for intimacy's sake, but an intimacy that results in the 'exaltation' of men and women. God seeks nothing for himself, for he needs nothing from us. Everything he gives us is a free gift, with no strings attached. God's driving force, what moves him to act, is the good of people. To describe this, San Juan uses a word that he greatly cherished—'*engrandecer*', often translated in English as to 'exalt'. In Spanish, it literally means to enlarge, to make bigger, to change something or someone from good to great, or, echoing the words of the apostle Paul, 'from glory to glory' (2 Corinthians 3:18, KJV) until we achieve 'the full stature of Christ' (Ephesians 4:13, NRSV).

The sole reason why God seeks women and men is to *engrandecer* them—to make them greater, better and fuller human beings. John writes in one of his commentaries:

> Because we said that God makes use of nothing other than love, it may prove beneficial to explain the reason for this before commenting on the poem. The reason is that all our works and all our trials, even though they be the greatest possible, are nothing in the sight of God. For through them we cannot give him anything or fulfil his only desire, which is the *exaltation* of the soul. Of these other things he desires nothing for himself, since he has no need of them. If anything pleases him, it is the *exaltation* of the soul. Since there is no way by which he can *exalt* her more than by making her equal to himself, he is pleased only with her love. For the property of love is to make the lover equal to the object loved.[47]

This echoes the poem *Night*, in which, after the loved one has left the house and gone into the night, she finds the Beloved and they make love. In that intimate act, John unveils the mystery of the union as the loved one is transformed in the Beloved. We will explore the notion of transformation in Chapter 7. At this point, suffice it to say that John's picture of God is of a passionately loving and generous God who believes in us and goes out of his way to seek us, to meet us and to exalt our souls.

God as a loving 'mother'

Given the special place that women had in John's life, it is not surprising that he used a positive feminine image for God in some of his commentaries. One of those instances is found in *Living Flame of Love*, where he uses the indirect metaphor of 'mother' for God, and of 'child' for the person (soul) who does not wish to be led by God in the spiritual journey.

> It will happen that while God persists in keeping the soul in that silent quietude, it persists in its desire to act through its own efforts... It resembles a little boy who kicks and cries, wanting to walk when his mother wants to carry him; thus he neither allows his mother to make any headway nor makes any himself.[48]

A similar illustration is used at the beginning of the *Ascent of Mount Carmel*, comparing God with a mother.[49] In an even more explicit way, in his commentary on the *Dark Night*, San Juan uses the image of the *amorosa madre*, the 'loving mother', who feeds her child at each stage of the journey with the appropriate food. He writes:

> God nurtures and caresses the soul, after it has been resolutely converted to his service, like a loving mother who warms her child with the heat of her bosom, nurses it with good milk and tender food, and carries and caresses it in her arms. But as the child grows older, the mother withholds her caresses and hides her tender love; she rubs bitter aloes on her sweet breast and sets the child down from her arms, letting it walk on its own feet so that it may put aside the habits of childhood and grow accustomed to greater and more important things.'[50]

These examples show, as Colin Thompson observes, 'that a sixteenth-century friar is perfectly capable of moving outside a patriarchal framework as far as the conception of God is concerned, and that such language is rooted in Christian tradition, and needs to be recovered, not invented'.[51]

God as the 'God of surprises'

The poem *Spiritual Canticle* contains one of the most powerful and multi-layered pictures of God in its 14th song or stanza. This song marks a crucial moment in the poem. From here, the tone changes dramatically. The previous 13 stanzas have been about longing, aching, seeking and searching for the Beloved in all sorts of places. Song 14 assumes that an encounter has just taken place and that the union with the Beloved has been consummated, so the rest of the poem is full of songs of joy and fulfilment. These verses are an explosion of joy, celebration, delight and pleasure. It is not a self-centred, hedonistic pleasure but one that is centred on the Beloved, springing out of the love that the loved one feels for the Beloved, who is now all things to her. So here, the poet, speaking through the words of the bride, overwhelmed by this wonderful encounter, goes on to describe what the Beloved is to him. This song contains one of the most wonderful of John's depictions of God, through creation:

Mi Amado: las montañas,	My Beloved: the mountains,
los valles solitarios nemorosos	the wooded, solitary valleys,
las ínsulas extrañas,	the exotic islands,
los ríos sonorosos,	the resounding rivers,
el silbo de los aires amorosos.	the whistle of the lovely breezes.

I have deliberately kept both the Spanish original and the English translation side by side here, because this song is considered to be one of the finest-sounding poems in the Spanish language. The translation, although it conveys the meaning of the song, lacks some of the force and depth of the original.

What does the poet tell us about God in these words? To answer that question, we need to look at his commentary on this section of *Spiritual Canticle*. Here John explains the meaning of these images and what they say about God.[52]

'The mountains' are great, majestic, strong and beautiful. When the flowers are out they are full of colour, impregnated with lovely scents. 'This is the Beloved to me,' says John. As I write these words from the Sierra Nevada mountains, the same ones that San Juan saw from his convent cell in Granada, this image evokes very powerful ideas about God. On one level, the majestic mountains point to God's greatness and to our human smallness. They also convey a sense of shelter and safety, as a place where God can be felt and encountered. Connected also with John's experience of God, the mountains speak of a God who is higher than we can ever dream or imagine, hard to grasp and out of our reach.

'The valleys', John says, are tranquil, fresh and leafy, full of water that refreshes the soul, and full of life. 'This is my Beloved to me,' says John. But the valleys act as the counterpart to the mountains. The mountain is high; the valley is low. So, John suggests, God is so high that we cannot fully comprehend him and so low that we can never touch the bottom of his character with our limited minds.

'The exotic islands' are, literally, 'strange islands'. Although some people believe that the islands John describes may be those in the River Darro in Granada, it is clear from his commentary that he is referring to the strange, foreign islands of the New World. The *insulas extrañas* evoke the Central American and Caribbean islands, from which the Spanish conquistadors brought all sorts of new, exciting and exotic goods that Europeans had never seen or tasted before. To John, the Beloved is like those faraway islands, containing many new experiences, unpredictable and full of surprises.

The exotic islands are a warning to us about the dangers of trying to put God in a box. They encourage us to ensure that our images of God are not too small, too limiting or too constraining. They are a reminder that God will always be higher and deeper than we think, and always full of new things, ready to surprise us.

'The sounding rivers' is a metaphor for a source of life that fills and floods all else, whose sound silences all other sounds. This image resonates with the poem *Fountain* and the stream that runs and flows. 'This is my Beloved to me,' says John.

Finally, the Beloved is described as the 'whistle of the lovely breezes'. This image, John explains, describes God's gentle touch to our souls. Just as the air caresses our skin with its whistle, so God the Beloved caresses our souls, always in gentle ways. In other places, however, John will complain that, at times in life, that gentle caress can be felt as a hard slap.[53] This is particularly the case when God breaks into our mind as a beam of light: in order to make room for the light, he has to disentangle and pull apart all the neat boxes in which we have packed and wrapped our spiritual experiences. Those things no longer matter; they had a place once, but are no longer useful. This process, John says, causes great confusion and desolation in the mind. It is like a blow.

Through this list of images from nature and creation, John is suggesting something more profound about God, in line with his mystical tradition. He is saying that God is best known through experience rather than intellectual activity—in fact, that God may be experienced through all our senses and deep within our soul.

Encounter

Poems such as *Dark Night*, *Living Flame of Love* or the latter part of *Spiritual Canticle* cannot be understood outside of a deep and intimate encounter with God. Someone has said, 'It would be hard for John of the Cross to make up these phrases, if the starting point has not been the experience of a real encounter with God's Presence.'[54] One thing is clear when it comes to the experience of encounter: it is a gift from God, 'the work of his grace', as John says at the end of the poem *I entered where I knew not*, and cannot ultimately be put into words. In this sense, all our images of God are limited and imperfect. In another commentary, John writes:

> What God communicates to the soul in this intimate union is utterly ineffable, beyond the reach of all possible words—just as it is impossible to speak of God Himself so as to convey any idea of what He is—because it is God Himself who communicates Himself to the soul now in the marvellous bliss of its transformation.[55]

For John the mystic, it is in the intimacy of the encounter that God reveals his character fully to us, and the encounter shapes and informs our image of God. However, as we noted at the beginning of this chapter, John's picture of God as lover/mother/friend, drawn both from scripture and from the Christian tradition, also enables him to approach God with confidence and relate to God with intimacy. This is the God whom John invites us to seek, follow and encounter in the night—a God who seeks us first, lavishes his love on us and delights in making us better, fuller human beings.

For prayer and reflection

In your journey of faith, what has been your more common experience: seeking God, loving God and having faith in God, or being sought by God, loved by God and believed in by God?

What is your image or picture of God? If you were to draw, paint or write a story to illustrate who God is, what would it say?

Read prayerfully John's poem *Flame* (see page 103) and meditate on the various images of God the Holy Spirit in the poem.

Chapter 6

Creation: The connections with nature

Oh forests and deep thickets,
planted by the hand of the Beloved!
Oh meadows of green pastures,
painted with colourful flowers,
tell me if he has passed by you.

JOHN OF THE CROSS (*SPIRITUAL CANTICLE*, VERSE 4)

When we look at most of the spiritual giants, we see people who had a very special connection with nature. This was the case with Julian of Norwich in England, Francis of Assisi in Italy and John of the Cross in Spain. As mentioned in previous chapters, nature and creation played a very prominent role in John's poetry and spirituality. *Dark Night* and *Spiritual Canticle* are full of references to the Mediterranean landscape in which he grew up, very similar to the biblical scenery. Other poems, such as *Fountain* and *Flame*, draw from the symbolism of water and fire to describe God, and the *Romances on the Gospel* offer us a theology of creation deeply rooted in John's understanding of God. Much of the imagery in the *Romances* is borrowed from the book of Genesis, but some is from the first chapter of John's Gospel, to which it alludes.

In this chapter, I will explore in more detail the place of nature in San Juan's spirituality and the question of how our view of creation affects the way we relate to it. The mystic believes that nature and the entire universe are to be enjoyed and celebrated, for they are God's creation and reflect the glory of the Creator. They are also to be preserved and cared for, because 'they are planted by the hand of the Beloved' and reflect God's beauty.

San Juan draws his theology of creation from the first and the last books in the Bible. Inspired by the book of Genesis, he describes creation as being profoundly anthropocentric. As John sees it, God's first thought is to create human beings, and the rest of creation becomes the 'palace' in which people will live. Inspired by the book of Revelation, he uses the term 'bride' to describe not just the Church but humanity as a whole. So, in the *Romances*, he depicts the moment of creation as part of a conversation between the Father and the Son.

> *'Let it be done'—said the Father—*
> *'for your love deserves it.'*
> *And in saying these very words,*
> *he created the whole world.*
> *A palace for the bride,*
> *made in great wisdom,*
> *which contained two dwelling places,*
> *one above, and one below.* (Romances, *part 4*)

In the next part of the poem, John gives us a glimpse of the purpose of this 'palace' (creation), which is divided into two 'dwelling places', the heavens and the earth.

> *Those above possessed*
> *the Groom, in joy.*
> *Those below, in hope*
> *and faith infused by him,*

telling them that one day
he would exalt them
and that their life below
would be raised on high…
because he in every way
would become like one of them;
he would come to be with them
and with them would live and dwell
and so God would be man,
and man would be God. (Romances, part 4)

The physical act of creation, to San Juan's mind, is deeply connected with the historical event of the incarnation—the coming of Christ—and with the spiritual act of re-creation and transformation, which we will explore in Chapter 7. It is in the light of this wider context that he addresses the question of how we relate to nature and to the entire universe.

Seeing creation through God

John has been criticised by some for offering too negative a view of creation. In his commentaries, especially the *Ascent of Mount Carmel* and the *Dark Night*, there seem to be some warnings against delighting in nature or enjoying creation too much. Instead, he seems to encourage a more ascetic life of denial, through the disciplines of the active night of the senses and of the spirit. However, this is a caricature of San Juan's teachings, resulting from the selective reading of just one part of his writings. When we look at his works as a whole, we realise that his relationship with creation is, ultimately, a positive, affirming and life-giving one.

There are two moments in our relationship with nature,

according to John of the Cross. In the first moment, connected with the dark night, we need to 'deny' creation in order to focus on the Creator. The denial is connected with a need to redefine our relationship with nature, from the starting point of our relationship with God. In this respect, John says that what is important is to know creation through God, not God through creation. The warning he gives at this stage of the journey is consistent with his view of what it means to follow Christ: beware of the danger of creation taking the place of the Creator in your life. As Colin Thompson observes, 'His focus is on the way human desire becomes attached to created objects as substitutes for God, exploits them for its own satisfaction, and comes to regard them as ends in themselves, thereby disabling the soul from progressing towards her true fulfilment in God.'[56]

The second moment occurs when our relationship with God becomes intimate and transformative. John says that, in that process, our relationship with nature is also transformed. We begin to see nature through the eyes of God, rejoicing in its beauty and delighting in its gifts. Nature becomes what some theologians have called a 'sacrament of the encounter between human beings and their Creator'.[57] This is clear in the poem *Spiritual Canticle*, discussed in the previous chapter, when, out of the encounter with the Beloved, the loved one cries out with joy, 'My Beloved, the mountains...'. In the words that follow in the poem, the bride describes how she now sees nature as painting and recreating the face of the Beloved. This process is what the former Archbishop of Canterbury, Rowan Williams, has called a re-conversion to creation.[58]

We know that this understanding of our relationship with God and nature also affected John's teaching on prayer during his ministry. Gerald Brenan, in his book *St John of the Cross*, describes how John, as prior of the convent in Granada, would take the friars out for long rambles in the country.

> When asked why he did this he would answer dryly that it was because, if they were left too long within the walls of the priory, they would want to leave it. But this was not the only reason. He believed in teaching them to pray in two different manners, now fixing their minds on God to the exclusion of everything else and now calling on the sky and hills, the trees and plants (*toda la hermosura de las cosas*—all the beauty of created things), to praise Him.[59]

Seeing God through creation

In John's vision of the cosmos and the universe, once creation is seen by the soul through the lenses of God, it begins to fulfil a very unique role. Creation, John says, leads us to God. His great commentary, the *Ascent of Mount Carmel*, uses the image of a physical mountain as a spiritual metaphor for the place that leads to God. He goes even further, to assert that one of the purposes of creation is to 'awaken our love for God'. Commenting on the verse 'planted by the hand of the Beloved', from *Spiritual Canticle*, San Juan writes, 'Only the hand of God, her Beloved, was able to create this diversity and grandeur... This reflection on creatures, this observing that they are things made by the very hand of God, her Beloved, strongly awakens the soul to love him.'[60]

In a different commentary, talking about the sorts of things that can help us draw closer to God, he acknowledges that 'there are souls who are greatly moved toward God by sensible objects'[61]—in other words, by the beauty of creation around us. As the editors of John's complete works in English rightly note, 'with his artistic temperament, John probably experienced this himself'.[62]

It seems true, from the numerous accounts we have about John's life, that he found nature to be a very powerful vehicle for encountering God. His good friend Jerome of the Cross, a travelling companion on many occasions, declared that John 'was a friend of solitude and used to long for it, especially when he found himself in the countryside, by rivers or fountains, or under the open sky'.[63] He also said that 'whenever [San Juan] came across rivers, fountains, skies, or fields, he would turn to prayer and claimed to see in them a je ne sais quoi of God'.[64]

In Chapter 2, I introduced the idea of 'night' as a spiritual symbol in John's understanding of the Christian journey—in fact, as his overarching metaphor for life on this earth. In discussing his love of nature, we cannot ignore John's love for the 'night' as the backdrop with which to contemplate the wonders of the universe. A fellow friar, John of Saint Anne, tells of the times when he was invited by John to go out at night to observe the open Andalucian sky:

> Occasionally he would take me with him, and would
> tell me about the beauty of the night sky and the light
> of so many different stars… and about the harmony of
> the heavens and the great music they make with their
> movements. Then, his words would describe the higher
> heaven of the saints, which was full of wonder and beauty.[65]

Another example of the way John related to nature comes from his time in Granada. One day, he was walking by the

River Darro with some fellow friars. Noticing a few little fish swimming in the river, in an almost Franciscan fashion he called the friars at once, saying to them:

> 'Come here, my brothers, to see how these little animals and creatures of God are praising him, so that your spirits may be lifted! For, since they who have no understanding are praising God, how much more should we do so ourselves.' And saying these words he entered into prayer, and the friars left him there in contemplation.[66]

This profoundly biblical view of creation—depicted especially in the Psalms, where creation appears to be in conversation with God, praising and worshipping the Creator—is also rooted in Christian tradition. It inspired the early Church Fathers in their writings, medieval reform and pioneer leadership in Europe, and Christian Celtic spirituality in the British Isles. A wonderful example of the Celtic response is seen in the words of a Gaelic woman who describes how her mother taught her to worship God with the whole of creation.

> My mother would be asking us to sing our morning song to God… giving glory to the God of the creatures for the repose of the night, for the light of the day, and for the joy of life. She would tell us that every creature on earth here below and in the ocean beneath and in the air above was giving glory to the great God of the creatures and the worlds, of the virtues and the blessings, and would we be dumb![67]

Ecology and holistic spirituality

Although 'ecology' was not a word known or used by San Juan, there is no doubt that creation was central to his spirituality. Some theologians consider it the third pillar, or principle, of the spiritual journey.[68] However, this is not creation in isolation, but creation in relationship. The picture painted by John in his poems, especially *Spiritual Canticle*, is of the world as a community of living creatures that influence each other and enjoy reciprocal relationships. These creatures share the same space and the same Creator, and are called to live in harmony with their environment and their Creator. This essentially ecological view of creation has an impact on the way John thinks of and relates to nature.

In recent years, the Christian church, particularly in the West, has developed an increasing interest in ecology. This genuine concern for what has become known as the 'stewardship of creation' responds to the current issues threatening the planet, from global warming through to the unsustainable lifestyles connected with consumerism. A growing number of Christian groups are encouraging individuals and congregations to take practical steps to care for the environment and live more sustainable lives. Alongside these efforts, a 'green' or 'ecological' spirituality has emerged that is rooted primarily in the Genesis accounts of creation and our responsibility for the created world. In most of this literature, however, creation takes a subsidiary place and human beings are encouraged to relate to it in a vertical, top-down manner, as overseers who must ensure that God's handiwork is protected and preserved.

For the great women and men of faith, including John of the Cross, who had a high view of creation, their relationship with creation was not a vertical but a horizontal one. They recognised their interconnectedness with all things, celebrated the divine breath that gives life to all that is created, and viewed the entire universe as one big choir whose songs of praise we humans are invited to join.

That is the reason why John of the Cross did not detach the spiritual life from the ordinary life. Work and play were fully integrated in his spirituality. He lived his relationship with God as an all-encompassing, holistic reality that included his relationship with the rest of creation. The mystic is concerned with preserving the beauty of creation, not just so that it can continue to be fruitful but so that it can continue to praise the Creator. In this sense, as we have seen, it has great similarities to Celtic Christian spirituality.

The same John who wrote some of Spain's finest poetry and taught men and women some of Christian spirituality's deepest wisdom also loved nature in very practical ways. He got his hands dirty in the vegetable garden of the Granada convent, worked as a farmer in the summer of 1591 in the village of La Peñuela, helped to restore buildings and water channels in Granada and Segovia, and took pleasure in harvesting wheat and collecting chickpeas. His engagement with nature, with the outdoors, with creation, was a source of spiritual life. It energised him spiritually and drew him closer to the Beloved. As Rowan Williams puts it, San Juan regarded 'the purpose of nature as leading towards "supernature". The goal of the created order is to point the soul to self-transcendence.'[69]

For prayer and reflection

Augustine was one of the early Christian writers who described how nature and its beauty pointed him to God the Creator.

Read the following words and meditate on this conversation between Augustine and creation:

But what is my God? I put my question to the earth. It answered, 'I am not God', and all things on earth declared the same. I asked the sea and the chasm of the deep and the living things that creep in them, but they answered, 'We are not your God. Seek what is above us.' I spoke to the winds that blow, and the whole air and all that lives in it replied, 'Anaximenes [a sixth-century BC philosopher who taught that air was the first cause of all things] is wrong. I am not God.' I asked the sky, the sun, the moon and the stars, but they told me, 'Neither are we the God whom you seek.' I spoke to all the things that are about me, all that can be admitted by the door of the senses, and I said, 'Since you are not my God, tell me about him. Tell me something of my God.' Clear and loud they answered, 'God is he who made us.' I asked these questions simply by gazing at these things, and their beauty was all the answer they gave.[70]

Many people find 'prayer walks' a helpful way to connect with God through nature. These are silent walks in which we open our senses to the life around us in trees, plants, rivers, birds and other wildlife. In doing so, we recognise that nature was praising the Creator way before we were born, and that now we are invited to join creation in that worship of God.

If you are able, go for a prayer walk and write down your own encounters with God through creation.

Read Psalm 148 as an act of praise to God the Creator.

Chapter 7

Transformation: Becoming like the Beloved

Yet to all who did receive him, to those who believed in his name, he gave the right to become children of God.
JOHN 1:12

One of the sermons that has stayed with me from my days as a university student was delivered by a visiting preacher in my local church. His passage was John 1, and he began by asking a simple question: 'For what purpose were we created?' He was addressing the congregation of young men and women, mainly evangelical Christians. Many hands went up: 'To worship God and serve him through our lives.' Different variations on this response were articulated by a number of people—no doubt, a typical Sunday school textbook answer.

The preacher turned to the Bible and said, 'Tonight I want to share with you what the true purpose of life is, according to Scripture.' Then he read John 1:12: 'Yet to all who received him, to those who believed in his name, he gave the right to become children of God.' He paused for a moment and said, 'The purpose of life on earth is this: that we may *become* children of God.' The emphasis was on 'becoming', not being—a process or a journey that involves change and transformation. Although, in a sense, we are already God's children, by creation and adoption through baptism, there is another sense in which that reality has not yet been fully realised. Becoming children of God, the preacher explained, is a lifelong journey that involves leaving behind the things in our lives that are not life-giving in order to embrace God's life, growing thus into our full potential as human beings, into the full stature of Christ.

It was only years later, when I began to read John of the Cross, that I was able to make connections between this idea at the heart of the gospel and what Christian writers had been teaching for centuries. Ever since the first century, Christians have believed that we are called to a higher and deeper life in Christ that involves transformation. The end of that transformation is for human beings to eventually be *like* Christ. John, the Gospel writer, in his first letter says, 'Dear friends… what we will be has not yet been made known. But we know that when [Christ] appears, we shall be *like him*, for we shall see him as he is' (1 John 3:2, emphasis added).

Two generations after John wrote this letter, in the second century AD, Irenaeus, Bishop of Lyon, summed up the purpose of the incarnation in simple words: the Son of God became the Son of Man, so that the sons and daughters of men and women may become children of God.[71] Many centuries later, in 16th-century England, the Anglican bishop Lancelot Andrewes advocated the same principle. In one of his sermons he taught:

> Whereby, as before He of ours, so now we of His are made
> partakers. He clothed with our flesh, and we invested
> with His Spirit. The great promise of the Old Testament
> accomplished, that He should partake our human
> nature; and the great and precious promise of the New

76

[Testament], that we should partake his divine nature, both are this day accomplished.[72]

This is the wonderful mystery at the heart of spiritual formation—the transformation of the whole person as she partakes in Christ's divine nature and becomes more and more like the Beloved. The process has been given different names by different traditions within the church. In the West, both Catholic and Protestant theologians have connected it with the notion of 'sanctification'. In the Eastern Orthodox tradition, it has been known as 'deification' or *theosis*. In both cases, the image evokes the idea of humans becoming more and more like God.

Rowan Williams, commenting on John of the Cross's understanding of *theosis*, reminds us that John's fundamental question in spiritual formation was about personal motivation.

> The question put to the believer is about the ultimate
> direction of his or her life. For the sake of *what* do we live?
> If the answer to that is in terms of self-directed concern
> or finite matters in general, the human subject is failing
> to respond to the deepest vocation of its being, the call
> to 'likeness', the central paradox that human fulfilment is
> in going beyond the confines of the self and the tangible
> world to share the freedom of God.[73]

As we have explored in previous chapters, spiritual transformation is central to John's vision of the Christian journey through the dark night. The summit of the encounter between Beloved and loved one in his best-known poem, the *Dark Night*, makes this clear.

Oh, night that guided me,
oh, night more gentle than the dawn,
oh, night that united
Beloved and loved one,
loved one transformed in the Beloved! (Dark Night, *verse 5*)

This encounter with the Beloved, in San Juan's experience, changes everything. The intimate union with Christ marks the summit of a personal transformation that is present throughout the spiritual journey, yet is most present in this moment of union.

Becoming divine: the heavenly soul

In previous chapters we have touched on some aspects of the journey connected with the active night—that is, what *we* do in order to declutter our souls and allow God to meet with us in deeper, more meaningful ways. We have also explored some of the aspects of the passive night—that is, what *God* does in us to '*engrandecer*' our souls, by the Holy Spirit, through grace. Here the focus is on the ultimate manifestation of that passive night, of God's action in our soul, as we surrender ourselves to God's ways, God's presence and God's embrace. This process, for John, can have only one natural result—the transformation of the whole person in the divine image. In one of his commentaries he writes:

Accordingly, God makes the soul die to all that he is not, so that when it is stripped and flayed of its old skin, he may clothe it anew. Its youth is renewed like the eagle's [Psalm 103:5], clothed in the new self, which is created, as the Apostle says, according to God [Ephesians 4:24]. This renovation illumines the human intellect with supernatural light so it becomes divine, united with the divine; informs the will with love of God so it is no longer less than divine, and loves in no other way than divinely, united and made one with the divine will and love; and is also a divine conversion and changing of the memory, the affections, and the appetites according to God. And thus this soul will be a soul of heaven, heavenly and more divine than human.[74]

The language used by John here may seem somewhat unusual. This process of 'becoming divine' affects every aspect of our individual identity—the intellect, the will, the memory, the affections and the appetites. God is interested in renewing every aspect of our being. Every single part of who we are has to be reclothed in God's divine garments. Only then does the soul become a 'heavenly soul'.

It is important to clarify, at this point, how John understands the idea of 'becoming divine'. This process is his metaphor for our becoming one with God. It means not that we become only divine but that, like Christ, we will be one with God, both human and divine. In other words, the end of spiritual transformation is our union with God, our becoming one with the Beloved. It is about experiencing oneness with the source of life, as the natural result of a life that has grown in her single-hearted love of God (with all her heart, soul, mind and strength).

Also, this transformation does not mean that we become part of the essence of God. John does not believe that people lose their individual identities, merging with some abstract divine energy. San Juan's picture of God, as we saw in Chapter 5, is a deeply personal one, and so is his image of human beings. We are created unique, in the image of God, and we retain our uniqueness even after the transforming encounter with the Beloved has taken place. In union with God, our human nature, all that we are, is transformed as we become the person we were created to be in Christ. We become divine, as Lancelot Andrewes would say, by participation.

This idea is expressed poetically in John's *Romances on the Gospel*. There, he uses another metaphor to describe our becoming divine by participation. For him, Christ becomes human so that humans ('the bride') may live the divine life, as they partake in the life of the Trinity.

> *He [God the Son] would deal with them,*
> *with them he would eat and drink.*
> *And he would choose to come,*
> *and stay with human beings,*
> *until the time*
> *was fulfilled*
> *when together they'd rejoice*
> *in eternal melody...*
>
> *And so, just like the Father and the Son*
> *and the one who from them proceeds*
> *they each live in one other,*
> *so it would be with the bride,*
> *who in awe inside of God,*
> *the life of God she would live.* (Romances, *part 4*)

The 'already but not yet'

One of the biggest frustrations in the spiritual journey is the feeling that we are making no progress, that we are not really growing, changing or becoming 'better' followers of the Rabbi of Nazareth. At times, we feel as if we take one step forward and two steps back. We are acutely aware that our lives do not always match our words, and our words do not always match our faith. We feel far from becoming like Christ, as far as anyone can be from becoming a heavenly soul. Transformation is a beautiful idea, but when we look deep within ourselves the reality is not always pretty.

The Bible is full of people who felt just like that—men and women who set their hearts and minds on God and on doing God's work on earth, and struggled to get things right. Time and time again, these people, now considered heroes and heroines of the faith, got frustrated with their failure to move as fast as they wanted, impatient with their human weaknesses and hopeless about their personal brokenness. Yet, time and time again, God sees beyond the present moment into the future. He looks at the person that is, and sees the person that can be. God sees the potential in every person to be transformed into the likeness of Christ. When Jesus meets Simon the fisherman, he does not see just the stubborn, impulsive and outspoken man who stands before him. He sees a disciple, a witness to his cause and a future leader of his Church. Hence the words of Jesus on their first encounter: '"You are Simon son of John. You will be called Cephas" (which, when translated, is Peter)' (John 1:42). The ancient custom of renaming someone, in this instance and throughout the Bible, always points to a new identity of the person in relationship to God, and reflects God's faith in human beings and their potential to become more like him.

Age is no barrier to change. In Genesis, we are told that God sees the potential of an elderly couple to fulfil his purposes in their lives. So, when God looks at Abr-am (meaning 'great father'), he sees Abra-ham ('the great father of a multitude');

and when he looks at Sar-ai ('*my* princess', the princess of Abram's household and tribe), he sees Sar-ah ('*the* princess' who will have a bigger role in the history of humanity).

San Juan, too, was a great believer in the human potential to live the life of God on this earth, to become heavenly souls, to be transformed by the Beloved, into the Beloved. For him, partaking in 'the life of God' is not just a promise for the future, after death. It carries the possibility of a present reality. It can be experienced here and now, albeit in small, limited and imperfect ways. It is an 'already but not yet' scenario, described with great passion in his poem *Living Flame of Love*. Here, the poet begins to express a longing for a future consummation of full union with God,

> *Oh living flame of love*
> *that tenderly wounds in my soul*
> *its deepest centre!*
> *Since you no longer hide,*
> *if it is your will: finish now,*
> *and tear through the veil of this sweet encounter!*
> (Living Flame, *verse 1*)

However, as we continue to read, you realise that he has glimpsed and experienced this union before. He has already felt the presence of the Holy Spirit in his life, as a 'soft hand' and a 'delicate touch, that tastes of eternal life, and pays every debt!' (*Living Flame*, verse 2). The closing words of the poem evoke the picture found in *Dark Night*, where the union has been consummated between Beloved and loved one.

> *How gently and lovingly*
> *you wake up on my chest,*
> *where secretly you dwell alone;*

and in your fragrant breathing,
full of goodness and glory,
how tenderly you make me fall in love! (Living Flame, *verse 4*).

There are hints in these verses of an intimacy that is ongoing. It is neither just a past experience nor only a hoped-for future aspiration. The transformation, John says, begins here and now, and it is the work of the Holy Spirit, God's living flame of love, from beginning to end.

It is an 'already' reality, yes—but it has not yet been fully realised. Commenting on the opening verse of *Spiritual Canticle*, 'Where did you hide?', San Juan explores the idea of the hiddenness of God experienced during this earthly life versus the possibility of encountering, seeing, tasting and being changed by God into the likeness of the Beloved. Union and transformation by and into the Beloved on this earth is possible. However, it will not be complete until our earthly journey is over. In John's own words:

> Though in this mortal life the soul will never reach to
> the interior secrets as it will in the next, however much
> she may hide herself... she will reach to such perfection
> here, as to be united, and transformed by love, in the
> Son of God, its Bridegroom. So effectually will this be
> wrought that the soul will feel itself so united to Him,
> so learned and so instructed in His secrets, that, so far
> as the knowledge of Him in this life is concerned, it will
> be no longer necessary for it to say: 'Where did you hide
> yourself?'[75]

John's realism about the Christian journey, with the challenges and difficulties at the heart of the dark night, is balanced with a sense of faith in the human potential to be 'transformed by love, in the Son of God', here and now.

For prayer and reflection

Nature as an enacting parable

There are many signs of transformation in the world around us. As we explored in Chapter 6, nature provides us with a wonderful array of examples of change, growth and transformation—from the seasons of the year to the cycle of life in seeds that become plants, that grow to maturity, that bear fruit containing new seeds to generate new life. In this sense, nature may be seen as enacting a parable that points to something beyond itself—the human potential to be transformed into heavenly souls.

You may wish to go for a prayer walk and reflect on your own transformation as you contemplate the signs of change in nature around you.

Jesus himself used images from nature to illustrate the mystery of transformation at the heart of God's kingdom. Read the parable of the mustard seed and meditate on the story (Matthew 13:31–32).

The Lord's Supper as an enacted parable

Jesus told many parables that captured the imagination and pointed people to God. On his last night with his disciples, on the eve of his death, he gathered with the Twelve to celebrate the Passover meal. This last supper turned into a parable of his own life (given for us), of events still to come (his death and resurrection), and of a new renaming. Taking bread, Jesus said, 'This is my body, given for you.' Taking the cup, Jesus said, 'This is my blood, shed for you.'

From that moment, this enacted parable became the way his

followers would remember him for generations to come. It also became a parable that spoke of transformation, as bread and wine become spiritual food and drink.

One of the ways in which John of the Cross, as a priest and a follower of Jesus, met with the Beloved in a special and tangible way was in the breaking of bread. At the end of the poem *Fountain*, he writes:

That everlasting fountain hidden is
within this living bread to give us life,
although by night.

All creatures are summoned to these waters.
Here they drink in darkness and have their fill,
because it is night.

This life-giving fountain I desire,
which in the living bread I contemplate,
although by night.

Next time you take Communion, meditate on this act of worship as an enacted parable of transformation. Reflect on how these ordinary gifts that are normally used to sustain our physical bodies are set aside and, by God's grace, become spiritual food to sustain our spiritual lives. Reflect also on how taking part in this meal that speaks of divine transformation can nurture your personal transformation into the likeness of the Beloved.

Chapter 8

Love: The beginning and end of the journey

And where there is no love, put love, and you will draw out love.
ST JOHN OF THE CROSS[76]

All that has been said so far in previous chapters, and all the teachings and poems of San Juan, could be summed up in the above statement. John wrote these words from Madrid toward the end of his life. They were addressed to a nun from Segovia, Mother María Encarnación, who, like John, knew what it was like to be rejected, persecuted and ill-treated by her sisters. She knew the challenges of living in community while remaining faithful to Jesus' command to love our neighbour. This challenge is particularly poignant when the people with whom we share our lives think differently or are different from us.

For John, the answer to resolving conflict in a community is not to win people through arguments or persuade them with words, but to identify where love is lacking and to inject love into those places and situations. The church would be wise to apply this simple principle to so many of its current debates, divisions and conflicts.

'Love divine, all loves excelling'

The reason why, for John, 'love' is the answer not just to conflict resolution but to the whole of life on this earth is that God (as another John affirmed) 'is love, and all who live in love live in God, and God lives in them' (1 John 4:16, NLT). John of the Cross has taught us that God is the seeker, the lover and the exalter of human beings. Now he teaches us that God is also the initiator of the love story in which we are caught up. God's love, not ours, marks the beginning of our journey to him.

In one of his commentaries, John uses the biblical story of the love between two men, Jonathan and David, to illustrate our union with God and the primacy of the divine love. With his usual passion, he writes:

> This union is more wonderful than all that can be said of it. Scripture mentions something about it in reference to Jonathan and David. The love Jonathan bore David was so intimate that it knitted his soul to David's [1 Samuel 18:1]. If the love of one man for another was so strong, what will be the tie caused through the soul's love for God, the Bridegroom; especially since God here is the principal lover, who in the omnipotence of his fathomless love absorbs the soul in himself, more efficaciously and forcibly than a torrent of fire would devour a drop of morning dew! [77]

God is 'the principal lover'. To love is God's principal activity. All that God does, all that God is, can be summed up in this one word (a verb and noun), 'love'. In his poetry, John describes God in terms of love. The Holy Spirit is the Living

Flame of Love. Jesus, the Son, is the Beloved, echoing the title given to him in the fourth Gospel. The Father is the lover, '*el amante*', who lavishes his love on the Son and, out of love, makes all that exists, for the Son. Every person of the Trinity is moved by love, exists by love and delights in loving. As Iain Matthew puts it, 'About love, John makes two things really clear, and these are what we want to say here. One, that love is something God does; it is, first, his activity. And, two, that his love changes a person.'[78]

Love at the beginning of the journey

When Jesus was asked about the greatest commandment, he quoted the words of the Shema, from Deuteronomy 6:5: 'Love the Lord your God with all your heart and with all your soul and with all your strength.' Then he added another important command, taken from Leviticus 19:18: 'Love your neighbour as yourself.' This summary of the Law of Moses, recorded in Matthew 22:36–40, got the approval of those who were enquiring of Jesus. It also became the foundation for the Christian way of life. Loving God with all that we are and all that we have, and loving others as ourselves, became the lens through which all other laws, rules and commandments were to be understood. Love was and is the measuring rod against which all else is measured.

It should not surprise us, therefore, that San Juan, in his Letter 13, said that 'the activity of the will, which is to love God, concentrates the affection, joy, pleasure, satisfaction, and love of the soul only on God, leaving aside all things and loving him above them all'. This radical invitation to walk on the road less travelled, leaving behind all that is not of God in our lives, in order to love God with an undivided heart, marks for John the beginning of the journey through the night.

We see this in some of his poems. In *Dark Night*, the soul starts the journey to the Beloved, leaving the house, 'on fire, with love's deepest yearnings'. In *Spiritual Canticle*, the activity of the entire poem (the search, the finding and the sexual intimacy) is driven by love. The human being, in both these poems, is defined by the language of love. The person is the '*amada*', the 'loved one', while God, in Christ, is known as the '*Amado*', the 'Beloved'. In both cases, the love language used is a passive one. The emphasis is on being loved by the other—we by God, first; and God by us, second.

This use of mutually passive language is very telling. It speaks of the human experience of letting go of our fears and insecurities and abandoning ourselves to be loved, touched, caressed, kissed, possessed, by another. It speaks of becoming vulnerable as we are loved, for in the act of intimacy one cannot hide anything from the other. All the loved one can do is to receive and enjoy the love that is freely given. So it is with our relationship with God, says John.

The mutually passive language also points to something deeper and more significant. San Juan sees a mutuality in our relationship with God. Yes, God initiates the love story, but, without our response of love, there is no continuing story. This crucial idea is sadly lost in many of the current translations of John's poetry into English, including the 'official' one in the Carmelite edition of John's complete works.[79] Here the Beloved is translated as the 'Lover', stressing the active role of God in the relationship yet missing something of the mutuality described above.

Because love is the most powerful, life-giving drive in life, love is the most transforming energy in our spiritual journey.

As we saw in Chapter 4, at the beginning of the journey and throughout, love is central to our prayer life. 'If you can love, you can pray,' John would say, for if we truly love God, we will be able to communicate with him naturally and freely. This opens up a door of new and great possibilities for those who seek God from the margins of institutional religion. For those who find 'church' difficult, yet wish to grow spiritually in their lives, a love-based spirituality has a universal dimension and appeal. In describing the way that John invites spiritual seekers to follow, Colin Thompson notes how that new path made a huge impact on certain Christians in 16th-century Spain. He writes:

> To follow [this spiritual path] only love is required, and all have the capacity for loving, regardless of the level of their knowledge or intellectual accomplishment. Time and time again one comes upon statements to the effect that those excluded from power and education (the poor and simple, women) can travel this road—even, presumably, the illiterate, as long as they are well guided. Theirs is a spirituality for the marginalised, an alternative to the inaccessibility and the sterility of the religion of the established order, the world in which the clerks (men) studied scholastic theology, in Latin, and disputed abstruse theological questions. Mystical literature in this tradition opened up a way of prayer and growth in the Christian faith for those who were not content with a merely superficial practice, yet lacked the qualifications for deeper study.[80]

The mystical or contemplative path affects the way that we relate to God. Until the twelfth century, Christian spirituality had put its emphasis on 'knowing' God with one's head, as a cerebral exercise. In the twelfth century, four centuries before San Juan, with the emergence of St Bernard's Cistercian spirituality in France, a great shift took place. The way to union with God was no longer based on what people 'knew', but on whom they 'loved'. God is to be sought with the heart, not just with the head, so all that we are and all that we have must join forces in loving the God who has loved us first. This is an experiential form of spirituality, rooted in a mutual relationship of love with God, which is able to change us from inside out.

When love hurts

We all experience pain in our lives as a result of loving someone. It could be the pain of accompanying someone we love through a difficult time, due to ill health, financial problems or the break-up of a relationship, or it could be the deep void caused by seeing a loved one fade away and die. We all know that the more we love someone, the more it hurts when we know they are hurting. That is one of the unavoidable realities of living and loving.

One person who knew well how much love can hurt was Jesus of Nazareth. In his life and death, he embodied real love in deeply human ways. In Jesus we see a love that touches the untouchables, brings healing to the broken and rebels against the injustices of his day. We also see a love that is selfless, that is prepared to make itself vulnerable, that is generous in giving, to the point of giving up life itself so that others might live. This is the love that invites us to walk the extra mile, to love the person who makes our life difficult, to give generously even if it hurts—especially when it hurts.

For John of the Cross, that is what love is about. He does not advocate an emotion-based, feeling-driven type of love. In *Sayings of Light and Love*, he wrote, 'Love consists not in feeling great things, but in having great detachment and in suffering for the Beloved' (Saying 115). Real, life-changing love is always sacrificial and has very practical implications for the way we live our lives. It is a selfless love that follows the example of Jesus' selfless existence and is rooted in one of his most challenging teachings—about loving one's enemy, whether our 'enemy' is someone we have fallen out with, a person who actively opposes us or simply someone we find difficult. Real love is not easy and can, at times, be painful, but John knows very well, from his own experience, that there is no other way to grow as human beings into the full stature of Christ.

This love-in-action idea permeates John's teachings and writings. In his commentary on *Spiritual Canticle*, he appeals to 1 Corinthians 13 to describe the practical nature of a love that never gives up and endures all things, a love that is not just about feelings but about actions. 'Those who truly love God,' he concludes, 'must strive not to fail in this love.'[81] John Bell, from the Iona Community, agrees with San Juan in affirming that the sort of love described by Paul in the Corinthians passage 'is not simply about following the dominant emotion, it is also about exercising sensitivity and choice'.[82] Later in life, in a letter written to a nun, John of the Cross encouraged her to love others even when it hurts, because selfless love has the power to change people. 'Show great love for those who contradict and fail to love you,' he wrote, 'for in this way love is begotten in the heart that has no love. For that is how God acts with us, loving us so that we may love him through the love he lavishes on us.'[83]

One of the greatest examples of that sacrificial love in John's own life comes from the days leading to his death in Úbeda, in 1591. There, Crisóstomo, the prior of the community, went out of his way to make John's life (and death) as difficult and painful as possible. His antagonism toward John led to inhumane treatment. The mystic remained calm and forgiving throughout, showing his love to the prior, even when loving was painful—and, toward the very end of his life, something happened. Just as San Juan was about to die, Crisóstomo fell on his knees by John's bedside and, weeping and sobbing, begged his forgiveness. It was a change of heart caused by John's relentless love.

There is another way in which love can be experienced as a painful reality. For John, God's touch in our lives, through the Holy Spirit, can cause a 'love wound' that only God can heal. In his teaching, he likens the wound caused by God's love to the wounds created by the surgeon when operating on a person to remove something bad and make the person healthy again. Those wounds and scars are unavoidable and necessary. They speak of the healing and new life experienced by the previously sick person. So it is with the wound of love that occurs when God, as a surgeon, operates in our soul. In that sense, the wound is beautiful and life-giving. In one of his commentaries, John wrote:

O happy wound, wrought by one who knows only how to heal! O fortunate and most blessed wound; you were made only for the delight and gratification of the soul! You are great, because he who caused you is great! And your delight is great because the fire of love is infinite and makes you delightful. O, then, delightful wound, so much more sublimely delightful the more the cautery touched the intimate centre of the soul, burning all that was burnable in order to give delight to all that could be delighted![84]

It is unpopular nowadays to talk about a God whose love can cause us pain, even a wound in our lives. We want to experience the love without having to put up with the pain. Yet, for San Juan, the way of love walked by Jesus was the way of the cross. Allowing God to declutter within us all that is not life-giving, 'burning all that is burnable', can be a painful experience, but it is essential if we seek to grow in our spiritual life. It is not all 'doom and gloom', John says, for the same wound that causes the pain also brings the freedom, the healing and the joy that our soul longs for.

The end of the journey

In both *Dark Night* and *Spiritual Canticle*, the end of the journey for the loved one, or bride, is the intimate union with the Beloved. This love union, charged with sensual language, stands as the summit of each poem. Love is the driving force that has moved the loved one to seek the Beloved, not as a passive but as an active force in the relationship. In John's words, 'It is something wonderful that since love is never idle, but in continual movement, it is always emitting flames here and there like a blazing fire.'[85] Love's power has also transformed the loved one into the Beloved: one has changed into the other. Love is at the beginning and at the end of the spiritual journey, and love is its beginning and end.

The John who, out of love for God and others, embarked on a journey of transformation as a priest and reformer of his Christian communities is the same John who endured im-

94

prisonment, a campaign of libel from his Carmelite brothers and inhumane treatment during the sickness that led to his death. It was out of this experience of loving and being loved, and the pain and frustration caused by that love, that the poet wrote some of the most amazing poetry in the Spanish language. In the words of Ian Matthews, 'This is John at his most real. His God is poetry. Love for his God, and for the people of his God, is John's passion. In some parts of his writing, John can be difficult, apologetic. But in speaking of love, his confidence is absolute. He knows what he is talking about.'[86]

It is also out of that experience of loving and being loved that San Juan affirms the centrality of love in a person's faith journey. Love, John believes, turns spiritual formation into spiritual transformation. Love alone can change us into the person that God created us to be.

Finally, love is the rule by which we will be 'judged' at the end of our journey on this earth. In fact, John does not use the verb 'to judge' when talking about the afterlife. He prefers to think of it as a loving examination. 'When evening comes, you will be examined in love,' he wrote (*Sayings of Light and Love* 60). In other words, in the evening of our life, when we come face to face with our Creator, God will not be interested in how many books on Christian spirituality we have read, how many church services or Bible studies we have attended, or how successful or unsuccessful we were in our business or career. The Beloved will be interested in how much we loved, how selfless our love was, and how many people we touched with that love. That will be the final test, and that should be our ultimate motivation for life and for living.

For prayer and reflection

Some of the greatest women and men of God have lived this love-based spirituality holding a newspaper in one hand and a Bible in the other (as Karl Barth put it)—the reality of the world in which they live informing their reading of scripture, and vice versa.

Read the news in a local paper or online, prayerfully, trying to identify the places where there is no love in the world, your country or your community. Pray for love to fill those loveless situations and for God to show you ways in which you can practically inject love into at least one of those places.

Then, allow God's living flame of love to rekindle your love for God and others, by reading afresh the hymn of love in 1 Corinthians 13. Ask the Holy Spirit to empower you to live the sort of love Paul describes in this passage.

Selected poems
with translations

Noche Oscura

1. En una noche oscura,
   con ansias en amores inflamada,
   (¡oh dichosa ventura!)
   salí sin ser notada,
   estando ya mi casa sosegada.

2. A oscuras y segura,
   por la secreta escala disfrazada,
   (¡oh dichosa ventura!)
   a oscuras y en celada,
   estando ya mi casa sosegada.

3. En la noche dichosa,
   en secreto, que nadie me veía,
   ni yo miraba cosa,
   sin otra luz ni guía
   sino la que en el corazón ardía.

4. Aquésta me guïaba
   más cierta que la luz del mediodía,
   adonde me esperaba
   quien yo bien me sabía,
   en parte donde nadie parecía.

5. ¡Oh noche que me guiaste!,
   ¡oh noche amable más que el alborada!,
   ¡oh noche que juntaste
   amado con amada,
   amada en el amado transformada!

6. En mi pecho florido,
   que entero para él solo se guardaba,
   allí quedó dormido,
   y yo le regalaba,
   y el ventalle de cedros aire daba.

Dark Night

1. On a dark night,
   on fire with love's deepest yearnings,
   oh, blessed chance,
   unnoticed I left my home,
   my house being now all stilled.

2. In darkness and secure,
   down the secret ladder, disguised
   oh, blessed chance!
   in darkness and concealment,
   my house being now all stilled.

3. In that blessed night,
   in secret, for no one saw me,
   I did not look around,
   with any other light or guide,
   save the one that burned within my heart.

4. That light guided me
   more surely than the light of noonday
   to where I was awaited _to where he lay waiting for me_
   by him I knew so well,
   in a place where no one appeared.

5. Oh, night that guided me, _'oh guiding night'_
   oh, night more gentle than the dawn,
   oh, night that united
   Beloved and loved one,
   loved one transformed in the Beloved!

6. Upon my flowery chest, _'Flowering breast'_
   which I kept solely for him alone, _How He lay sleeping_
   there he fell asleep, _which I kept for him_
   and I caressed him, _alone_
   whilst the cedars with their fanning made a breeze.
   and I embraced him

7. El aire de la almena,
   cuando yo sus cabellos esparcía,
   con su mano serena
   en mi cuello hería,
   y todos mis sentidos suspendía.

8. Quedéme y olvidéme,
   el rostro recliné sobre el amado,
   cesó todo, y dejéme,
   dejando mi cuidado
   entre las azucenas olvidado.

Fonte

Qué bien sé yo la fonte que mane y corre,
aunque es de noche.

1. Aquella eterna fonte está escondida,
   que bien sé yo do tiene su manida,
   aunque es de noche.

2. Su origen no lo sé, pues no le tiene,
   mas sé que todo origen de ella tiene,
   aunque es de noche.

3. Sé que no puede ser cosa tan bella,
   y que cielos y tierra beben de ella,
   aunque es de noche.

4. Bien sé que suelo en ella no se halla,
   y que ninguno puede vadealla,
   aunque es de noche.

5. Su claridad nunca es oscurecida,
   y sé que toda luz de ella es venida,
   aunque es de noche.

7. The breeze from the turret
   when I parted his hair;
   with his serene hand,
   my neck he wounded
   and all my senses he suspended.

8. There I stayed and forgot myself,
   my face I reclined on the Beloved.
   everything ceased and I abandoned myself,
   leaving my cares
   among the lilies forgotten.

*And when the breeze
blew in from the forest,
Blowing back our hair
He wounded my soul
With his gentle hand
suspending all my
senses.*

*leaving all my cares
forgotton with the lillies
of the field.*

Fountain

How well I know the fountain that springs and flows
although by night.

1. That eternal fountain is hidden,
   how well I know from where its source flows,
   although by night.

2. Its origin I know not for it has none,
   yet this I know, all origin from it derives,
   although by night.

3. I know there cannot be something so fair,
   and that earth and heavens drink from there,
   although by night.

4. I know there is no ending to this fountain,
   and that no one may traverse its waters,
   although by night.

5. Its clarity can never be obscured,
   and I know that all light from it shines,
   although by night.

6. Sé ser tan caudalosos sus corrientes.
   que infiernos, cielos riegan y las gentes,
   aunque es de noche.

7. El corriente que nace de esta fuente
   bien sé que es tan capaz y omnipotente,
   aunque es de noche.

8. El corriente que de estas dos procede
   sé que ninguna de ellas le precede,
   aunque es de noche.

9. Aquesta eterna fonte está escondida
   en este vivo pan por darnos vida,
   aunque es de noche.

10. Aquí se está llamando a las criaturas,
    y de esta agua se hartan, aunque a oscuras
    porque es de noche.

11. Aquesta viva fuente que deseo,
    en este pan de vida yo la veo,
    aunque es de noche.

Llama

1. ¡Oh llama de amor viva
   que tiernamente hieres
   de mi alma en el más profundo centro!
   Pues ya no eres esquiva
   acaba ya si quieres
   ¡rompe la tela de este dulce encuentro!

2. ¡Oh cauterio süave!
   ¡Oh regalada llaga!
   ¡Oh mano blanda! ¡Oh toque delicado

6. I know its flooding current is so mighty;
   that it waters hell and heavens and humanity,
   although by night.

7. The current that from this fountain is born,
   I know well of its power and its force,
   although by night.

8. The current that proceeds from these two,
   I know is not preceded by the other,
   although by night.

9. That everlasting fountain hidden is
   within this living bread to give us life,
   although by night.

10. All creatures are summoned to these waters.
    Here they drink in darkness and have their fill,
    because it is night.

11. This life-giving fountain I desire,
    which in the living bread I contemplate,
    although by night.

Flame

1. Oh living flame of love
   that tenderly wounds in my soul
   its deepest centre!
   Since you no longer hide,
   if it is your will: finish now,
   and tear through the veil of this sweet encounter!

2. Oh gentle cautery!
   Oh gracious wound!
   Oh soft hand! Oh delicate touch

que a vida eterna sabe
y toda deuda paga!
Matando, muerte en vida has trocado.

3. ¡Oh lámparas de fuego
en cuyos resplandores
las profundas cavernas del sentido,
que estaba oscuro y ciego,
con estraños primores
color y luz dan junto a su querido!

4. ¡Cuán manso y amoroso
recuerdas en mi seno
donde secretamente solo moras,
y en tu aspirar sabroso
de bien y gloria lleno,
cuán delicadamente me enamoras!

Entréme donde no supe

Entréme donde no supe:
y quedéme no sabiendo,
toda ciencia trascendiendo.

1. Yo no supe dónde estaba,
pero, cuando allí me vi,
sin saber dónde me estaba,
grandes cosas entendí;
no diré lo que sentí,
que me quedé no sabiendo,
toda ciencia trascendiendo.

2. De paz y de piedad
era la ciencia perfecta,
en profunda soledad

that tastes of eternal life
and pays every debt!
In killing, you have changed death into life.

3. Oh lamps of fire!
   in whose beams of light,
   the deep caverns of the senses,
   once obscure and blind,
   now give forth, with strange flares,
   warmth and light by their Beloved's side.

4. How gently and lovingly
   you wake up on my chest,
   where secretly you dwell alone;
   and in your fragrant breathing,
   full of goodness and glory,
   how tenderly you make me fall in love!

I entered where I knew not

I entered where I knew not
and there I remained unknowing,
all knowledge transcending.

1. I knew not where I was,
   yet, when I saw me there,
   not knowing where I was,
   I understood great things.
   I shall not say the things I felt,
   all I can say is that I remained unknowing,
   all knowledge transcending.

2. Perfect this knowledge was,
   full of peace and full of mercy,
   in deep solitude, I knew,

entendida, vía recta;
era cosa tan secreta,
que me quedé balbuciendo,
toda ciencia trascendiendo.

3. Estaba tan embebido,
tan absorto y ajenado,
que se quedó mi sentido
de todo sentir privado,
y el espíritu dotado
de un entender no entendiendo.
toda ciencia trascendiendo.

4. El que allí llega de vero
de sí mismo desfallece;
cuanto sabía primero
mucho bajo le parece,
y Su ciencia tanto crece,
que se queda no sabiendo,
toda ciencia trascendiendo.

5. Cuanto más alto se sube,
tanto menos se entendía,
que es la tenebrosa nube
que a la noche esclarecía:
por eso quien la sabía
queda siempre no sabiendo,
toda ciencia trascendiendo.

6. Este saber no sabiendo
es de tan alto poder,
que los sabios arguyendo
jamás le pueden vencer;
que no llega su saber
a no entender entendiendo,
toda ciencia trascendiendo.

that this was the way of blessing.
It was such a secret thing,
that there I remained stammering,
all knowledge transcending.

3. I felt so very drunk,
so absorbed and alienated,
that my senses lost all sense,
and there my spirit remained,
and was granted, I know not how,
a new wisdom, yet unknowing,
all knowledge transcending.

4. Those who truly reach this place,
they now die unto themselves.
All they understood before,
seems to them, too low a knowledge,
and his knowledge growing in them,
means they remain there unknowing,
all knowledge transcending.

5. The higher that one ascends,
the less one understands,
for this cloud, though it be dark,
brightens the night with its light.
And so, those who knew it before,
always remain unknowing,
all knowledge transcending.

6. This knowledge of unknowing
has such high power and strength,
that the wise in their thinking
can never win with their heads;
for their knowledge never seems
to understand this unknowing,
all knowledge transcending.

7. Y es de tan alta excelencia
   aqueste sumo saber,
   que no hay facultad ni ciencia
   que la puedan emprender;
   quien se supiere vencer
   con un no saber sabiendo,
   irá siempre trascendiendo.

8. Y, si lo queréis oír,
   consiste esta suma ciencia
   en un subido sentir
   de la divinal esencia;
   es obra de su clemencia
   hacer quedar no entendiendo,
   toda ciencia trascendiendo.

Cantico Espiritual (CB)

Canciones entre el alma y el Esposo

Esposa

1. ¿Adónde te escondiste,
   Amado, y me dejaste con gemido?
   Como el ciervo huiste,
   habiéndome herido;
   salí tras ti clamando, y eras ido.

2. Pastores, los que fuerdes
   allá por las majadas al otero:
   si por ventura vierdes
   aquel que yo más quiero,
   decidle que adolezco, peno y muero.

7. And this high form of knowledge
   is such an excellent way,
   that no human power or might,
   can ever reach to its depth.
   Those who surrender themselves
   to this knowing of unknowing
   will always in life transcend.

8. For those who have ears to hear,
   this high knowledge consists
   of a feeling, oh so deep,
   of the divine Being.
   This is the work of his grace,
   leaving us there not knowing,
   all knowledge transcending.

Spiritual Canticle

Songs between the soul and the Bridegroom

Bride

1. Where did you hide,
   Beloved, and left me crying?
   You fled like the stag,
   having wounded me.
   I left searching for you, and you were gone.

2. Shepherds, you who climb up
   to the hilltops with your flocks:
   If by chance you see
   him whom I love the most,
   tell him that I am hurting, crying, dying.

3. Buscando mis amores,
   iré por esos montes y riberas;
   ni cogeré las flores,
   ni temeré las fieras,
   y pasaré los fuertes y fronteras.

Pregunta a las criaturas

4. ¡Oh bosques y espesuras,
   plantadas por la mano del Amado!
   ¡Oh prado de verduras,
   de flores esmaltado!
   Decid si por vosotros ha pasado.

Respuesta de las criaturas

5. Mil gracias derramando
   pasó por estos Sotos con presura,
   e, yéndolos mirando,
   con sola su figura
   vestidos los dejó de su hermosura.

Esposa

6. ¡Ay, quién podrá sanarme!
   Acaba de entregarte ya de vero:
   no quieras enviarme
   de hoy más ya mensajero,
   que no saben decirme lo que quiero.

7. Y todos cuantos vagan
   de ti me van mil gracias refiriendo,
   y todos más me llagan,
   y déjame muriendo
   un no sé qué que quedan balbuciendo.

8. Mas ¿cómo perseveras,
   ¡oh vida!, no viviendo donde vives,

3. Looking for my love,
   I will walk through these mountains, by these rivers,
   I will not pick the flowers,
   nor will I fear the beasts,
   and I will cross through fortresses and borders.

She asks the creatures
4. Oh forests and deep thickets,
   planted by the hand of the Beloved!
   Oh meadows of green pastures,
   painted with colourful flowers!
   Tell me if he has passed by you.

The creatures reply
5. Pouring a thousand graces
   he hurrily passed by these groves,
   and after looking at them,
   solely by his presence
   he clothed them with his beauty.

Bride
6. Ah! Who will be able to heal me?
   Give yourself to me at once,
   do not send me any more messengers
   today, for none can tell me
   what I want to know.

7. And those who freely wander
   a thousand graces tell me about you now,
   they wound me even more,
   and leave me here dying
   of something I know not, in their stammering.

8. And, how you endure,
   oh life!, not living where you live,

y haciendo porque mueras
las flechas que recibes
de lo que del Amado en ti concibes?

9. ¿Por qué, pues has llagado
   aqueste corazón, no le sanaste?
   Y, pues me le has robado,
   ¿por qué así le dejaste,
   y no tomas el robo que robaste?

10. Apaga mis enojos,
    pues que ninguno basta a deshacellos,
    y véante mis ojos,
    pues eres lumbre dellos,
    y sólo para ti quiero tenellos.

11. Descubre tu presencia,
    y máteme tu vista y hermosura ;
    mira que la dolencia
    de amor, que no se cura
    sino con la presencia y la figura.

12. ¡Oh cristalina fuente,
    si en esos tus semblantes plateados
    formases de repente
    los ojos deseados
    que tengo en mis entrañas dibujados!

13. ¡Apártalos, Amado,
    que voy de vuelo!

Esposo

Vuélvete, paloma,
que el ciervo vulnerado
por el otero asoma
al aire de tu vuelo, y fresco toma.

but dying by the arrows
received
by that which you conceive of the Beloved.

9. Why, if you my heart have wounded,
have you not brought your healing?
And since you stole my heart,
why did you leave it thus,
not taking what you stole along the way?

10. Extinguish you my anger,
for no one else can do it.
And let my eyes now see you,
for you set them aflame,
and I want them to be for you alone.

11. Unveil to me your presence,
and let the sight of your beauty kill me.
For love-ache
cannot be healed,
except by your presence and your image.

12. Oh crystal-clear fountain,
if in this, your silver shining face,
you could suddenly show me
the long-desired eyes,
which are sculpted in my heart!

13. Turn them away, Beloved,
I am flying away!

Bridegroom

Return, my dove,
for the wounded stag
is appearing over the hill
fanned by your wings, enjoying the breeze.

Esposa

14. Mi Amado, las montañas,
    los valles solitarios nemorosos,
    las ínsulas extrañas,
    los ríos sonorosos,
    el silbo de los aires amorosos,

15. la noche sosegada
    en par de los levantes del aurora,
    la música callada,
    la soledad sonora,
    la cena que recrea y enamora.

16. Cazadnos las raposas,
    que está ya florecida nuestra viña,
    en tanto que de rosas
    hacemos una piña,
    y no parezca nadie en la montiña.

17. Detente, cierzo muerto;
    ven, austro, que recuerdas los amores,
    aspira por mi huerto
    y corran sus olores,
    y pacerá el Amado entre las flores.

18. ¡Oh ninfas de Judea!,
    en tanto que en las flores y rosales
    el ámbar perfumea,
    morá en los arrabales,
    y no queráis tocar nuestros umbrales.

19. Escóndete, Carillo,
    y mira con tu haz a las montañas,
    y no quieras decillo;
    mas mira las compañas
    de la que va por ínsulas extrañas.

Bride

14. My Beloved: the mountains,
    the wooded, solitary valleys,
    the exotic islands,
    the resounding rivers,
    the whistle of the lovely breezes,

15. The quiet night,
    awaiting the sunrise,
    the silent music,
    the sounding solitude,
    the love-enticing supper.

16. Hunt for us the foxes,
    for our vineyard is now in blossom,
    meanwhile with many roses
    let us make a bouquet,
    and let no one appear in the mountain.

17. Stop and die, north wind,
    come and reignite love, south wind,
    breathe through my garden,
    let its aromas flow,
    and the Beloved will eat among the flowers.

18. Oh nymphs of Judea!
    Since the fragrance of the amber
    now fills the flowers and the roses,
    stay there in the outskirts,
    do not wish to enter our home.

19. Hide away, my dear,
    and look, turning your face to the mountains.
    Do not say a word.
    Instead, look at the company
    of her, who goes through exotic islands.

El Esposo

20. A las aves ligeras,
    leones, ciervos, gamos saltadores,
    montes, valles, riberas,
    aguas, aires, ardores,
    y miedos de las noches veladores:

21. Por las amenas liras
    y canto de sirenas, os conjuro
    que cesen vuestras iras,
    y no toquéis al muro,
    porque la esposa duerma más seguro.

22. Entrado se ha la esposa
    en el ameno huerto deseado,
    y a su sabor reposa,
    el cuello reclinado
    sobre los dulces brazos del Amado.

23. Debajo del manzano,
    allí conmigo fuiste desposada;
    allí te di la mano,
    y fuiste reparada
    donde tu madre fuera violada.

Esposa

24. Nuestro lecho florido,
    de cuevas de leones enlazado,
    en púrpura tendido,
    de paz edificado,
    de mil escudos de oro coronado.

25. A zaga de tu huella
    las jóvenes discurren al camino
    al toque de centella,

The Bridegroom

20. I say to the light-winged birds,
    lions, deer, climbing goats,
    mountains, valleys, rivers,
    waters, winds, flames,
    and fears of the waking nights:

21. By the lovely lyres
    and the song of sirens, I conjure you
    to cease all your anger
    and not to touch the wall,
    so that the bride in safety may sleep.

22. The bride has now entered,
    in the pleasant longed-for garden,
    and delighting there she rests,
    her neck reclined,
    on the sweet arms of the Beloved.

23. Beneath the apple-tree,
    there we consummated our love,
    there I held your hand,
    and thus you were restored,
    where your mother had been raped.

Bride

24. Our flowery bed,
    knitted by dens of lions,
    stretched out in purple,
    strengthened by peace,
    crowned with a thousand golden shields.

25. Following your footprints,
    the young women walk along the path,
    at the touch of a spark,

al adobado vino;
emisiones de bálsamo divino.

26. En la interior bodega
de mi Amado bebí, y, cuando salía,
por toda aquesta vega,
ya cosa no sabía,
y el ganado perdí que antes seguía.

27. Allí me dio su pecho,
allí me enseñó ciencia muy sabrosa,
y yo le di de hecho
a mí, sin dejar cosa;
allí le prometí de ser su esposa.

28. Mi alma se ha empleado
y todo mi caudal en su servicio;
ya no guardo ganado,
ni ya tengo otro oficio,
que ya sólo en amar es mi ejercicio.

29. Pues ya si en el ejido
de hoy más no fuere vista ni hallada,
diréis que me he perdido,
que, andando enamorada,
me hice perdidiza y fui ganada.

30. De flores y esmeraldas,
en las frescas mañanas escogidas,
haremos las guirnaldas
en tu amor florecidas,
y en un cabello mío entretejidas.

31. En sólo aquel cabello
que en mi cuello volar consideraste,
mirástele en mi cuello
y en él preso quedaste,
y en uno de mis ojos te llagaste.

to taste the spiced wine,
juices of divine balm.

26. In the inner wine cellar
    of my Beloved I drank, and, when I left
    walking out into country,
    I no longer knew anything,
    and I lost the flock I cared for.

27. There he gave me his chest,
    and taught me a wisdom full of flavour.
    There I gave myself to him
    fully, keeping nothing to myself;
    there I promised to be his bride.

28. My soul and all my heart
    are dedicated now to his service,
    I no longer keep a flock,
    and have no other call,
    for now, to love alone is my sole occupation.

29. If from now on,
    I was no longer seen here in the common,
    you will say I went missing,
    that, because I was in love,
    I lost myself and then was found.

30. With flowers and emeralds,
    picked and gathered in the cool mornings,
    we shall make the garlands
    flowering in your love,
    and woven in my hair.

31. Only by that hair,
    which you gazed flying on my neck,
    as you saw it there,
    you were captivated,
    and were wounded by one of my eyes.

32. Cuando tú me mirabas,
    tu gracia en mí tus ojos imprimían;
    por eso me adamabas,
    y en eso merecían
    los mios adorar lo que en ti vían.

33. No quieras despreciarme,
    que, si color moreno en mí hallaste,
    ya bien puedes mirarme
    después que me miraste,
    que gracia y hermosura en mí dejaste.

Esposo

34. La blanca palomica
    al arco con el ramo se ha tornado,
    y ya la tortolica
    al socio deseado
    en las riberas verdes ha hallado.

35. En soledad vivía,
    y en soledad ha puesto ya su nido,
    y en soledad la guía
    a solas su querido,
    también en soledad de amor herido.

Esposa

36. Gocémonos, Amado,
    y vámonos a ver en tu hermosura
    al monte y al collado,
    do mana el agua pura;
    entremos más adentro en la espesura.

37. Y luego, a las subidas
    cavernas de la piedra nos iremos,
    que están bien escondidas,

32. When you looked at me, with your eyes,
    your grace was imprinted in my whole being.
    For that reason you loved me,
    and thus my eyes deserved
    to worship what they saw in you.

33. Do not despise me now,
    for, if you found in me a dark skin,
    now you can look again,
    for, the first time that you looked,
    your beauty and your grace on me you lavished.

Bridegroom

34. The white sweet little dove
    has returned with the branch to the ark,
    and the little turtledove
    has found the longed-for mate
    by the green rivers.

35. In solitude she lived,
    in solitude she made her nest.
    In solitude she is guided,
    alone by her Beloved,
    who, also in solitude, is wounded by love.

Bride

36. Let us rejoice, Beloved,
    and let us go and contemplate your beauty
    in the mountain and the hill,
    by the pure water spring.
    Let us enter deep into the thicket.

37. And then, we shall climb up
    to the high caves in the rocks,
    which are so well concealed,

y allí nos entraremos,
y el mosto de granadas gustaremos.

38. Allí me mostrarías
aquello que mi alma pretendía,
y luego me darías
allí tú, ¡vida mia!,
aquello que me diste el otro día:

39. el aspirar del aire,
el canto de la dulce filomena,
el soto y su donaire
en la noche serena,
con llama que consume y no da pena

40. Que nadie lo miraba;
Aminadab tampoco parecía,
y el cerco sosegaba,
y la caballería
a vista de las aguas descendía.

Romances Sobre el Evangelio 'In principio erat Verbum', acerca de la Sanctíssima Trinidad

I

En el principio morava
el Verbo y en Dios vivía
en quien su felicidad
infinita posseýa.
El mismo Verbo Dios era
que el principio se dezía
él morava en el principio
y principio no tenía.

and there we shall go in,
and delight in the juice of pomegranates.

38. There you would show me
that which my soul had been seeking,
and then, you, my life,
would give me there
that which you gave me the other day:

39. The breathing of the air,
the song of the sweet nightingale,
the forest in all its beauty,
in the tranquil night,
with a flame that consumes yet gives no pain.

40. No one looked at him;
nor did Aminabad appear,
and the quiet siege,
and the cavalry
descended at the sight of the waters.

Romances on the Gospel 'In principio erat Verbum', about the Holy Trinity (extracts)

I

In the beginning the Verb
dwelt and lived in God
in whom he possessed
infinite happiness.
The very Verb God was
who is mentioned at the beginning.
In the beginning he dwelt
and beginning he had none.

Él era el mismo principio
por eso dél carecía
el Verbo se llama Hijo
que del principio nacía.
Ale siempre concevido
y siempre le concevía
dale siempre su sustancia
y siempre se la tenía.
Y assí la gloria del Hijo
es la que en el Padre avía
y toda su gloria el Padre
en el Hijo posseýa.
Como amado en el amante
uno en otro residía
y aquese amor que los une
en lo mismo convenía.
Con el uno y con el otro
en ygualdad y valía
tres personas y un Amado
entre todos tres avía

(…)

De la comunicación de las tres Personas
II
En aquel amor inmenso
que de los dos procedía
palabras de gran regalo
el Padre al Hijo dezía (…)
—Nada me contenta, Hijo,
fuera de tu compañía.
Y si algo me contenta
en ti mismo lo quería

He was the very beginning
and all beginning he lacked.
The Verb was named Son
and from the beginning he came to birth.
He had always conceived him
and continued to conceive him.
Always he gave him his nature
a nature he always possessed.
And thus, the Son's glory
was the one found in the Father
and all his glory the Father
bestowed upon the Son.
As beloved in the lover
the one dwelt in the other
and the love that unites them
agreed in all things.
With one and with another
in equality and worth
three persons and one Beloved
there were three with all of them

(…)

Of the communion of the three Persons
II
Out of the immense love
which proceeded from the two
words of great delight
the Father said to the Son (…)
Nothing fills me with happiness, Son,
outside from your company.
And if something made me happy
I would want that in yourself

el que a ti más se parece
a mi más satisfazía.

Y el quen nada te semeja
en mí nada hallaría
en ti solo me e agradado
¡o vida de vida mía!.
Eres lumbre de mi lumbre
eres mi sabiduría
figura de mi substancia
en quien bien me complazía.
Al que a ti te amare Hijo
a mí mismo le daría
y el amor que yo te tengo
ésse mismo en él pondría
en razón de aver amado
a quien yo tanto quería.

De la creación
III
—Una esposa que te ame
mi Hijo darte quería
que por tu valor merezca
tener nuestra compañía
y comer pan a una mesa
del mismo que yo comía
porque conozca los bienes
que en tal Hijo yo tenía
y se congracie conmigo
de tu gracia y loçanía.
—Mucho lo agradezco Padre,
—el Hijo le respondía—
a la esposa que me dieres

for the more someone is like you
the more joy they bring to me.

And the less they look like you,
nothing they will find in me.
Only in you, I am well pleased,
oh life of my life!
You are light of my light
you are my very wisdom
figure of my substance
in you I am well pleased.
To those who love you, Son,
I would give my very self,
and the love I have for you
I would lavish on them too
for they loved the very one
I have loved so very much.

Of creation
III
A wife that would love you Son
I would like to give to you
one that for your sake was worthy
to enjoy our company
to eat bread at our table
the same bread that I eat
that she may know the blessings
that I possess in my Son
and with me, she might rejoice
at your beauty and your grace.
—I am very grateful Father,
the Son answered him—
to the wife that you gave me

yo mi claridad daría
para que por ella vea
quánto mi Padre valía
y cómo el ser que posseo
de su ser lo recevía.

IV

—Hágase pues —dixo el Padre—,
que tu amor lo merecía.
Y en este dicho que dixo
el mundo criado avía.
Palacio para la esposa,
hecho en gran sabiduría
el qual en dos aposentos
alto y baxo dividía.

Los de arriva posseýan
al Esposo en alegría
los de abaxo en esperança
de fee que les infundía
diziéndoles que algún tiempo
él los engrandecería
y que aquella su baxeza
él se la levantaría
de manera que ninguno
ya la vituperaría
porque en todo semejante
él a ellos se haría
y se vendría con ellos
y con ellos moraría
y que Dios sería hombre
y que el hombre Dios sería
y trataría con ellos
comería y bebería

I would give my very light
that through it she might see
how wonderful my Father is
and how my very being
I have received from him.

IV

Let it be done, said the Father,
for your love deserves it.
And in saying these very words,
he created the whole world.
A palace for the bride,
made in great wisdom
which contained two dwelling places
one above, and one below.

Those above possessed
the Groom, in joy.
Those below, in hope
and faith infused by him,
telling them that one day
he would exalt them
and that their life below
would be raised on high
so that no one evermore
would mock it again,
because he in every way
would become like one of them;
he would come to be with them
and with them would live and dwell
and so God would be man,
and man would be God.
God would deal with them,
with them he would eat and drink.

y que con ellos contino
él mismo se quedaría
hasta que se consumase
este siglo que corría
quando se gozaran juntos
en eterna melodía
porque él era la cabeça
de la esposa que tenía
a la qual todos los miembros
de los justos juntaría
que son cuerpo de la esposa,
a la qual él tomaría
en sus braços tiernamente
y allí su amor le daría
y que assí juntos en uno
al Padre la llevaría
donde del mismo deleite
que Dios goza gozaría
que como el Padre y el Hijo
y el que dellos procedía
el uno vive en el otro
assí la esposa sería
que dentro de Dios absorta
vida de Dios viviría.

(...)

Del Nacimiento
IX
Ya que era llegado el tiempo
en que de nacer avía
assí como desposado
de su tálamo salía,

And he would choose to come
and stay with human beings,
until the time
was fulfilled
when together they would rejoice
in eternal melody.
For he was the head
of the bride
and in her all of the members
of the righteous would be one
being the body of the bride,
whom he would possess
holding her gently in his arms
giving her there his love
so that being together one
he would take her to the Father
where she would enjoy the same joy
that is enjoyed by God.
And so, just like the Father and the Son
and the one who from them proceeds
they each live in one other,
so it would be with the bride,
who in awe inside of God,
the life of God she would live.

(...)

Of the Birth
IX
The time had now arrived
for the baby to be born
as a groom from his wedding chamber
he came out

abraçado con su esposa
que en sus braços la traýa
al qual la graciosa madre
en un pesebre ponía
entre unos animales
que a la sazón allí avía
los hombres dezían cantares
los ángeles melodía
festejando el desposorio
que entre tales dos avía
pero Dios en el pesebre
allí llorava y gimía
que eran joyas que la esposa
al desposorio traýa
y la madre estava en pasmo
de que tal trueque veýa
el llanto del hombre en Dios
y en el hombre el alegría
lo qual del uno y del otro
tan ajeno ser solía.

embracing his wife
holding her in his arms.
The gracious mother
placed him in a manger
amongst some animals
that happened to be there.
Men sang canticles divine,
angels melodies unknown,
celebrating the marriage
consummated by these two.
But God, in the manger,
there, he wept and cried.
These were the jewels that the bride
brought to her wedding day.
Whilst the mother, in amazement,
watched this awesome exchange
the weeping of man in God
and in man the divine joy,
which in both cases
used to be so very rare.

Bibliography

Books

Biblioteca de Mística Carmelitana (Editorial Monte Carmelo), various volumes.

Gerald Brenan, *St John of the Cross, His Life and Poetry* (Cambridge University Press, 1975).

Kieran Kavanaugh and Otilio Rodriguez (trans.), *The Collected Works of Saint John of the Cross* (ICS, 1991).

Iain Matthew, *The Impact of God* (Hodder & Stoughton, 2010).

Paul Murray, *I Loved Jesus in the Night: Mother Teresa of Calcutta* (Paraclete Press, 2008).

Antonio T. de Nicolás, *St John of the Cross: Alchemist of the soul* (Weiser, 1996).

José Antonio Págola, *El Camino Abierto por Jesús* (Desclée, 2011).

Maria del Sagrario Rollán, *Vamos a ver en tu hermosura* (Editorial de Espiritualidad, 1989).

Colin Thompson, *St John of the Cross: Songs in the Night* (SPCK, 2002).

Rowan Williams, *The Wound of Knowledge* (Cowley, 1990).

Articles and papers

Alfonso Baldeón, 'Para este fin de amor fuimos creados', unpublished paper.

Baldomero Jiménez Duque, 'El Encuentro con Dios de Juan de la Cruz' (*Revista San Juan de la Cruz*, 20, 1997).

Antoni Klupczynski, *La Bondad de la Creación en San Juan de la Cruz* (Universidad de Navarra, 1997).

José Vicente Rodríguez, 'Las Grandes Líneas de la Espiritualidad Sanjuanista' (89th Capitulum Generale Ordinis Carmelitarum Discalceatorum, 2003).

José Vicente Rodriguez, 'San Juan de la Cruz y la Ecología' (*Revista de Espiritualidad*, 182, Madrid, 1987).

Notes

1 Dichos de Luz y de Amor, in Gerald Brenan, *St John of the Cross: His life and poetry* (Cambridge University Press, 1975), p. 99.

2 These Jewish communities are known as 'Sefardi' Jews, named after 'Sefarad', the name they gave 'Spain' in the 15th century.

3 The term 'evangelical' here means inspired by and centred on the gospel.

4 In prison he wrote the two *Romances*, *Fonte* and *Spiritual Canticle*.

5 See his Foreword to the commentary on *Spiritual Canticle*, addressed to Mother Ana de Jesús, written in Granada in 1584, pp. 582–83.

6 *Biblioteca Nacional Madrid*, ms. 8568, fol. 297.

7 Robert Frost, 'The road not taken', first published in *Mountain Interval* (Henry Holt, 1920). Available in *The Collected Poems* by Robert Frost (Vintage Classics, 2013). May also be accessed online.

8 Iain Matthew, *The Impact of God* (Hodder & Stoughton, 2010), p. 52.

9 Matthew, *Impact of God*, p. 55.

10 Colin Thompson, *St John of the Cross: Songs in the Night* (SPCK, 2008), p. 79.

11 See Paul Murray, *I Loved Jesus in the Night: Mother Teresa of Calcutta* (Paraclete Press, 2008).

12 Thompson, *St John of the Cross*, p. 79.

13 *1 Night*, Pt. 2:2–3

14 *1 Night*, 12:1.

15 Thompson, *St John of the Cross*, p. 220.

16 Sam to Frodo, in *The Lord of the Rings: The Fellowship of the Ring* dir. Peter Jackson (New Line Cinema/Wingnut Films, 2001)

17 Thompson, *St John of the Cross*, p. 98.

18 *Night*, verse 1.

19 *I entered where I knew not*, verse 1.

20 *Spiritual Canticle*, verses 1, 2, 3, 13.

21 *The Dark Night*, book 2, stanza 14, verse 2. Author's translation.

22 Although Juan de la Cruz never uses this word, the metaphor of decluttering conveys many of the ideas expressed by John in his commentaries, *The Ascent of Mount Carmel* and *The Dark Night*.

23 Quoted by José Antonio Págola, *El Camino Abierto por Jesús* (Desclée, 2011), p. 99.

24 *The Ascent of Mount Carmel*, book 3, chapter 17, verse 2.

25 *Ascent*, book 3, chapter 28, verse 2.

26 *Ascent*, book 3, chapters 30—45.

27 *The Living Flame of Love*, stanza 4, paragraph 6.

28 Antonio T. de Nicolás, *St John of the Cross: Alchemist of the soul* (Weiser, 1996), p. 184.

29 *Ascent*, book 3, chapter 12, verse 1.

30 *Ascent*, book 2, chapter 24, verse 8 (emphasis added).

31 Thompson, *St John of the Cross*, p. 138.

32 Address of Pope Paul VI, Closing General Meeting of the Second Vatican Council (7 December 1965).

33 *Living Flame*, stanza 3, verse 32.

34 *Ascent*, book 3, chapter 3, verse 5.

35 *Living Flame*, stanza 1, verse 33.

36 See the prologues to the commentaries *Ascent of Mount Carmel*, 2; *Spiritual Canticle*, 4; *Living Flame of Love*, 1.

37 See the testimony of Brother Juan Evangelista in *Biblioteca de Mística Carmelitana*, 10, p. 341.

38 José Vicente Rodríguez, 'Las Grandes Líneas de la Espiritualidad Sanjuanista' (CGOCD, 2003), p. 7.

39 Thompson, *St John of the Cross*, pp. 177–78.

40 *Sayings of Light and Love* 26 and 29.

41 *Spiritual Canticle* B, stanza 29, verse 3.

42 Alfonso Baldeón, 'Para este fin de amor fuimos creados', part 5, unpublished paper. The original Spanish reads: 'El corazón del hombre, hecho a la medida de Dios, no se satisface con menos que Dios.'

43 Although these two parables describe the kingdom of God, they are also regarded as metaphors for God's character.

44 *Biblioteca de Mística Carmelitana* 23, pp. 479–80.

45 *Living Flame*, stanza 3, verse 28.

46 *Ascent*, book 2, chapter 7, verse 3.

47 *Canticle*, stanza 28, verse 1 (emphasis added).

48 *Living Flame*, stanza 3, verse 3.

49 *Ascent*, prologue, verse 3.

50 *1 Night*, chapter 1, verse 2.

51 Thompson, *St John of the Cross*, p. 221.

52 *Canticle* B, songs 14 and 15, verses 1–21.

53 See *Night* commentary, chapter 5.

54 See Baldomero Jiménez Duque, 'El Encuentro con Dios de Juan de la Cruz', in *San Juan de la Cruz Journal* 20 (1997), p. 333.

55 *Canticle* B, song 26, verse 4.

56 Thompson, *St John of the Cross*, p. 189.

57 Maria del Sagrario Rollán, *Vamos a ver en tu hermosura* (Editorial de Espiritualidad, 1989), p. 33.

58 Rowan Williams, *The Wound of Knowledge* (Cowley, 1990), p. 188.

59 Brenan, *St John of the Cross*, p. 53.

60 *Spiritual Canticle* B, stanza 4, verse 3.

61 *Ascent of Mount Carmel*, book 3, chapter 24, verse 4.

62 Kieran Kavanaugh and Otilio Rodriguez, *The Collected Works of Saint John of the Cross* (ICS, 1991), p. 310.

63 Ms. Vat. 2862, fol. 8, quoted by José Vicente Rodriguez, 'San Juan de la Cruz y la Ecología', *Revista de Espiritualidad*, 182 (Madrid, 1987), p. 124. The Spanish reads: 'Era muy amigo de la soledad y suspiraba por ella, y más donde había campos amenos, ríos o fuentes, y si descubría el cielo en descampado.'

64 Ms. Vat. 2862, fol. 8. The Spanish reads: 'se ponía en oración y mirando los ríos, o fuentes, o cielos, o yerbas, en que decía ver un no sé qué de Dios.'

65 *Biblioteca Nacional de Madrid*, ms. 8568, 407. The Spanish reads: 'Llevábame algunas veces consigo, y luego trataba de la

hermosura del cielo y luz de tantas estrellas que decía que con ser tantas diferían en especie unas de otras y otras cosas de la armonía de los cielos y música que hacen grandísima con sus movimientos y luego iba subiendo hasta llegar al cielo de los bienaventurados, de allí decía lindezas de su hermosura.'

66 Ms. Vat. Sin. 25, page 56. Quoted by Rodríguez, 'San Juan de la Cruz y la Ecología', p. 127. The Spanish reads: '¡Vengan acá, hermanos, y verán cómo estos animalicos y criaturas de Dios le están alabando, para que levanten el espíritu, que pue, éstos sin entendimiento ni razón lo hacen, cuánta mayor obligación tenemos de alabarle nosotros. Y en esta plática se quedó suspenso, y los religiosos lo dejaron en su contemplación.'

67 Quoted in Seán Ó Duinn, *Where Three Streams Meet* (Columba Press, 2000), pp. 218–19.

68 Antoni Klupczynski, *La bondad de la creación en San Juan de la Cruz* (Universidad de Navarra, 1997), p. 316.

69 Williams, *Wound*, p. 176.

70 Augustine, *Confessions* ch. X, v.6, trans. R.S. Pine-Coffin (Penguin 1961), p. 212.

71 *Adv Haer* III 19,1.

72 Lancelot Andrewes, 'Sermons of the sending of the Holy Ghost preached upon Whit Sunday, Sermon 1' in Works, Sermons, Volume Three (Parker, 1841), pp. 107–129.

73 Williams, *Wound*, p. 176.

74 *Dark Night*, book 2, chapter 13, paragraph 11.

75 *Spiritual Canticle*, stanza 1, verse 10.

76 *Letter to Mother María Encarnación* (Madrid, 1591), no. 26.

77 *Spiritual Canticle*, stanza 31, verse 2.

78 Matthew, *Impact of God*, p. 110.

79 Kieran Kavanaugh and Otilio Rodriguez (trans.), *The Collected Works of St John of the Cross* (ICS, 1991). See also the poems translated by Antonio T. de Nicolás in *St John of the Cross: Alchemist of the soul*.

80 Thompson, *St John of the Cross*, p. 139.

81 *Spiritual Canticle*, stanza 13, verse 12.

82   John Bell, *Hard Words for Interesting Times* (WGP, 2003), p. 14.

83   Letter 33 to a Discalced Carmelite nun in Segovia, 1591 (author's translation).

84   *Living Flame of Love*, stanza 2, verse 8 (author's translation).

85   *Living Flame of Love*, stanza 1, verse 8 (author's translation).

86   Matthew, *Impact of God*, p. 109.

The Sacred Place of Prayer

The human person created in God's image

Jean Marie Dwyer, OP

Prayer is not a complicated set of methods or exercises, but as simple as living life, being ourselves and bringing God into our daily routine. Because we are all created in God's image, each of us is the privileged and sacred place of prayer.

Drawing on scripture, the desert tradition, great spiritual figures from history and the author's own Dominican tradition, this book explores the various steps we need to take to nurture our life in God. After laying the philosophical, biblical and theological groundwork, Sister Jean Marie Dwyer goes on to offer rich insights into how we find our true self and our place of belonging.

ISBN 978 0 85746 241 1   £7.99
Available from your local Christian bookshop or, in case of difficulty, direct from BRF: please visit www.brfonline.org.uk.

Also from BRF

Meditating with Scripture: John's Gospel

Using the ancient tradition of lectio divina

Elena Bosetti

'How should we read the Gospel of John? There are
so many ways. The one presented here is rooted in an
experience that does not separate reason from faith or the
intellect from the heart. It follows the method of lectio
divina, proposes a prayerful listening to the word and is
moved by the invocation of the Spirit. We cannot fly on
eagle's wings unless the Spirit lifts us.'

Using the ancient tradition of *lectio divina* ('sacred reading'),
this book leads us through John's Gospel, reflecting on the
people and events in the life of Jesus, as well as his teaching
and prayers, which combine to make this most carefully
structured and lyrical of Gospel accounts. Each chapter ends
with exercises to help us 'dialogue with the word' and a
prayerful meditation to help shape our response.

ISBN 978 1 84101 823 2   £7.99
*Available from your local Christian bookshop or, in case of difficulty,
direct from BRF: please visit www.brfonline.org.uk.*

Moments of Grace

Reflections on meeting with God

Joy MacCormick

From desolation to celebration, loneliness to love, *Moments of Grace* offers pithy, thought-provoking reflections on themes connecting God, faith and the journey of life. Questions for further pondering help the reader make links between head and heart, between what they believe, what they wrestle with believing and what they experience day by day.

Joy MacCormick, a New Zealand Anglican priest, has written this book to help people have a closer encounter with God in prayer, especially those who may struggle to find a place in conventional church worship.

ISBN 978 0 85746 224 4   £6.99
Available from your local Christian bookshop or, in case of difficulty, direct from BRF: please visit www.brfonline.org.uk.

Enjoyed
this book?

Write a review—we'd love to hear what you think.
Email: reviews@brf.org.uk

Keep up to date—receive details of our new books as they happen.
Sign up for email news and select your interest groups at:
www.brfonline.org.uk/findoutmore/

Follow us on Twitter @brfonline

By post—to receive new title information by post (UK only), complete
the form below and post to: BRF Mailing Lists, 15 The Chambers, Vineyard,
Abingdon, Oxfordshire, OX14 3FE

Your Details
Name _____
Address_____
_____
Town/City _____ Post Code _____
Email _____

Your Interest Groups (*Please tick as appropriate)	
☐ Advent/Lent	☐ Messy Church
☐ Bible Reading & Study	☐ Pastoral
☐ Children's Books	☐ Prayer & Spirituality
☐ Discipleship	☐ Resources for Children's Church
☐ Leadership	☐ Resources for Schools

Support your local bookshop
Ask about their new title information schemes.